noodle fusion

ASIAN NOODLE DISHES FOR WESTERN KITCHENS

Dorothy Rankin

W9-AWO-225

THE CROSSING PRESS
FREEDOM, CALIFORNIA

© 2000 Dorothy Rankin
Cover and interior design by Courtnay Perry
Cover photograph © 1999 Thompson + Narita
Interior photographs © 1999 Digital Stock on page 3, 31, 45, 53, 58, 63, 70, 92, 101, 109, 117,121, 131, 139, 155, 163, 189, 193, 199, 203, 221, 224.
Interior photographs © 1999 PhotoDisc on page 23, 24, 35, 39, 49, 67, 79, 135, 143, 145, 158, 179, 205.
Interior photograph by Dorothy Rankin on pages 69, 83, 195, 217.
Interior photographs © 1999 Thompson + Narita on page 7, 75, 107.
Printed in the USA

For information on bulk purchases or group discounts for this and other Crossing Press titles, please contact our Sales Manager at 800/777-1048.

Visit our Web site on the Internet: **www.crossingpress.com**

Library of Congress Cataloging-in-Publication Data
Rankin, Dottie.
     Noodle fusion : Asian noodle dishes for western kitchens / by
Dorothy Rankin.
         p. cm.
     ISBN 0-89594-956-3 (pbk.)
     1. Cookery (Pasta). 2. Noodles. 3. Cookery, Asian. I. Title.
TX809.M17R36   1999
641.8'22--DC21   99-33920
                                                                      CIP

Acknowledgments

To my favorite tasters

Laurie, Chris, Annie, and Sam

Many people gave me support and encouragement during the development of this book. My deepest thanks go to Laurie Pettibon, whose many useful suggestions in recipe development make this a better book, and whose computer skills frequently saved the day. I am most grateful to Amy Moody, who did a number of recipe tests and gave me much encouragement. And, to Linda Mansfield, for her enthusiasm, love of good food, and constant support. Thank you to Andy Thai of Thai Phat grocery for locating special ingredients.

I am especially indebted to Andrea Chesman, for her thoroughness, astute advice, vision, and guidance. Her recipe contributions have added immensely to this book. They are: Chicken Noodle Salad with Peanuts, Thai Grilled Beef and Rice Noodle Salad, Cold Soba Noodles and Vegetables, Pork Lo Mein, Summer Vegetable Salad with Cellophane Noodles, Thai-Style Crab Salad with Green Beans, Nuoc Cham, Southeast Asian Sweet and Sour Sauce, and Vietnamese Rice Noodle Salad with Shrimp. Thanks, Andrea, for your hard work and discerning palate.

Contents

Noodle
Know-How

WHEN I FIRST STARTED COOKING with Asian noodles, I had to go to Montreal or Boston for my supplies. Not so today. Not only are there specialty food stores nearby that cater to growing Vietnamese and Cambodian populations, there are all manner of ethnic foods in every supermarket—even in mostly rural Vermont. This is a change that is reflected in markets across the country. The global supermarket has truly arrived.

For cooks wishing to expand their repertoires of ethnic dishes, Asian noodles are a natural. Most of the noodle dishes are easy to prepare, light, and healthy to eat. If you use a light hand with chiles and chili paste, the dishes are unusually kid-friendly while remaining uniquely exotic. On the other hand, if it's spice you want, the cooking of Southeast Asia, Korea, and the Sichuan-style recipes can offer all the flavorful heat a jaded palate could crave.

Noodles have a long history in Asia. They are the original fast foods for working people, inexpensive and quick to make, easy to eat, nourishing, and filling. Everywhere you go in Asia, you will find street vendors and small shops selling inexpensive noodle dishes for an instant snack or light meal. If a squatting vendor with a small charcoal brazier can turn out delicious noodle dishes on the street, think what delicious meals you can turn out in your well-supplied kitchen!

Unlike Italian pasta, Asian pastas are made from a variety of flours, including wheat, rice flour, and buckwheat flour. In China, Korea, and Japan, wheat flour noodles may be made with and without eggs. Rice noodles, enjoyed throughout Southeast Asia and China, come in a variety of different widths. Pacific pastas are also made from mung bean and sweet potato starch.

Most of the Asian noodles available in the U.S. are sold dried. They can be stored in an airtight container for several months. Fresh noodles, which can be found where there are large Asian populations, should be stored in the refrigerator in their plastic wrappers for up to 5 days.

Like Italian pasta, Asian noodles dishes are quickly cooked. Most types of noodles are boiled briefly in plenty of salted boiling water, like Italian wheat pastas. They should be cooked until tender, then drained thoroughly. If the noodles have clumped together in the colander, they can be rinsed under running water. Some noodles, such as cellophane noodles, made from mung bean starch, require just a quick soak in hot water instead of boiling. Rice noodles may be boiled for use in cold dishes, or they may be softened in boiling water, then stir-fried to final tenderness.

There is very little standardizing in the packaging of noodles. For example, I can buy soba noodles in packages of 7.5 ounces and 8 ounces. I've specified 8 ounces of noodles in most recipes, but if your packages are a little over or a little under, don't worry about it—just use what you have. The same goes for cellophane noodles and any other noodles. Cooking these noodle dishes does not require precise measurements.

This lack of standardization also affects cooking times. If the noodles you purchase aren't exactly the same width of the noodles I use, the cooking times will vary. Therefore I have tried to give a range of times for when the noodles should be done. If you are cooking with an unfamiliar brand or type of noodles, start testing about a minute before the recipe says they should be done. Asian noodles should be cooked until they are completely tender to the bite— not al dente, but not mushy either.

In truth, the most difficult aspect of cooking Pacific Rim pastas is keeping all the different noodles straight. The same noodles go by different names in different countries.

NOODLE GLOSSARY

CELLOPHANE NOODLES

Also called bean threads, bean thread vermicelli, glass noodles, or transparent noodles, these noodles are made from the starch of mung beans. They are used extensively in Chinese and Southeast Asian cuisines. Uncooked, they are very thin, very brittle, white or transparent noodles. When softened (they don't require cooking, just soaking in hot water), they look translucent and have a slippery, soft, even gelatinous texture. They have very little taste and are used primarily to provide texture to a dish and to soak up the flavors. Look for them in packages with 8 separately wrapped 1.75-ounce or 2-ounce skeins or sleeves of noodles. (Note: In the recipes I call for 1.75-ounce skeins; a 2-ounce skein may be used instead without further adjustment to the recipe.)

To cook: Soak the bean thread noodles in hot tap water to cover until softened, about 15 minutes. For hot dishes, drain and proceed with the recipe. For cold dishes and salads, drain, rinse with cold water drain again, then proceed with the recipe.

If you want to use the noodles in short lengths, soften them first, then cut with scissors.

Warning! Cellophane noodles vary from brand to brand when it comes to soaking times. When you are trying out a new brand, you may wish to test the noodles at 5-minute intervals.

EGG NOODLES

Egg noodles are widely used in Asia and have many different names. Look for *mien* from China, *mee* from Thailand and Indonesia, *tamago somen* from Japan, *hokkien mie* from Malaysia and Singapore. Wheat-based egg noodles are available both fresh and dried, cut thick and thin. Fresh noodles may be found in the refrigerated case or freezer. If you buy or store your noodles frozen (they will keep for a month in the freezer), defrost the package before cooking. In American markets, you are most likely to find the thin Chinese egg noodles and the wider, flat Shanghai-type noodle. For the thin Chinese egg noodles, you can substitute fresh or dried Italian angel hair (cappellini) pasta, and for the wider, flat noodle, you can substitute linguine or fettuccine.

To cook: Boil in plenty of salted water until tender, about 4 to 5 minutes for dried egg noodles, and 3 to 4 minutes for fresh egg noodles, or according to the package directions. Use chopsticks to untangle the noodles as they cook.

SWEET POTATO STARCH GLASS VERMICELLI

Very similar in appearance and texture to cellophane noodles, sweet potato starch vermicelli is made from sweet potato starch instead of mung bean starch. Like cellophane noodles, sweet potato glass vermicelli have little flavor on their own, but do an excellent job of absorbing flavors from the sauce in which they are cooked. In fact, given the choice of mung bean cellophane noodles and sweet potato glass vermicelli, I go for the sweet potato noodles because they are somewhat thicker and plump up fatter than the cellophane noodles. They also have more substance and absorb sauce better. These noodles generally come in 10-inch lengths. If you want shorter lengths, break them before you proceed.

To cook: Cover the noodles with boiling water and set aside to soften for 10 minutes. Drain and rinse with cold water. Drain again.

RAMEN NOODLES

These crinkly wheat flour noodles are sold both fresh and dried under the name "ramen noodles." Noodle shops serve them in a steaming bowl of soup as a filling one-bowl meal, and they are also served stir-fried, as in yakisoba. Most commonly, you can find them sold in small, 2-serving packets with a seasoning envelope for use as an instant meal. Discard the seasoning packets, which usually contain MSG, and use the noodles with your own flavorings. Some stores carry larger packages of ramen noodles without the seasoning. These are worth seeking out.

To cook: Boil ramen noodles for 2 to 3 minutes, separating the strands and tasting them frequently until just done.

RICE NOODLES

Rice noodles come in a variety of shapes, from flat to round, and from thick to thin. They are typically sold in 1-pound packages with 3 to 4 skeins per pack. They are quite brittle when dry and become soft and slightly chewy when cooked. Unfortunately, since every rice noodle is called either rice stick or rice vermicelli, it is a little confusing to shop for the right noodle. You can judge rice noodles by appearance better than by labels.

Thin rice sticks/vermicelli are round and very thin (1/16 inch), similar to angel hair wheat pasta, but thinner and whiter in color. The wider, flat rice stick noodles known as *mi fen* (Chinese) or *bun* (Vietnamese) or *mihun* (Indonesian) are about 1/8-inch wide. These are the noodles of choice for pad Thai and pho.

To cook partially for stir-fries: Cover both thin rice vermicelli and fat rice stick noodles with boiling water and set aside to soak for 15 minutes. Drain well.

To cook completely for salads, spring rolls, etc.: Cook the noodles in a large pot of boiling water about 3 to 5 minutes. Drain and rinse well with cold water. The dried thin noodles can be deep-fried straight from the package as in mee krob. They instantly puff up into a huge crispy mass. Thicker (1/8-inch) rice noodles should be soaked in boiling water for 15 minutes, then brought to a boil for 30 seconds. Drain and rinse (for salads) or stir-fry until hot.

Soba Noodles

These thin, grayish-brown buckwheat noodles from Japan have a very distinctive, almost nutty flavor. Often found in health food stores, soba is touted as being rich in protein and fiber. Soba noodles are sold fresh or dried, plain or flavored, with additions such as powdered green tea (cha soba), lemon zest, lotus root, wild yam, mugwort, or black sesame seeds. They are served both hot and cold. In most recipes, soba and udon noodles can be used interchangeably.

The Japanese have two distinctively different methods for cooking noodles — boiling in the usual manner and the *sashimizu* method which cooks the noodles more evenly. You can cook soba noodles either way.

To cook: Bring a large pot of water to a boil, add the noodles, and cook for about 5 to 7 minutes until they are just tender. Drain and rinse.

To cook by the *Sashimizu* Method: Bring a large pot of water to a boil. Add the noodles and cook for 2 minutes. Add 1 cup of cold water and bring to a boil again. Repeat the procedure twice. Simmer the noodles until tender, about 5 minutes. Drain the noodles in a colander and rinse in cold water, rubbing the noodles together with your hands to remove the surface starch. The noodles will be evenly cooked this way.

Somen Noodles

Japanese fine wheat flour noodles are most often used in soups or served cold with a dipping sauce. In the Philippines, a very similar noodle is found, named *miswa*. Italian angel hair pasta (cappellini) makes a fine substitute.

To cook: Boil for about 5 minutes in plenty of boiling salted water. Cool under running water and drain thoroughly.

To cook by the *Sashimizu* Method: Bring a large pot of water to a boil. Add the noodles and stir. When the water returns to a boil, add 1 cup cold water. Taste a noodle. If it is not done, it will cook to a tender firmness shortly, so keep testing. Drain the noodles in a colander and rinse in cold water. Drain again.

Wheat Flour Noodles

There are many fresh and dried Chinese wheat noodles, some made with eggs (see above), and either round or flat in shape.

To cook: Boil in plenty of boiling salted water until tender, 5 to 7 minutes. Cool under running water and drain thoroughly.

UDON NOODLES

These flat or round, slippery wheat flour noodles from Japan are most often used in stews and soups. You can substitute soba or Chinese wheat flour noodles if you can't find udon.

To cook: Boil dried noodles for 10 to 12 minutes in plenty of boiling salted water. Fresh udon noodles will cook in about 2 to 2 1/2 minutes.

WRAPPERS

SPRING ROLL SKINS

Spring rolls are wrapped in a variety of wrappers. A thin, crepe-like wrapper goes by the name *lumpia* wrapper. In Southeast Asian cuisines, spring rolls may be wrapped in ultra-thin rice flour rounds. Spring roll wrappers are usually found frozen and should be defrosted in the refrigerator before you attempt to separate them and roll them. Avoid egg roll skins, which are thicker and tougher than spring roll skins. Spring rolls can be deep-fried or pan-fried.

RICE PAPER WRAPPERS

Vietnamese *banh trang* are round, semi-transparent crepes that are used for wrapping Vietnamese foods. Made from ground rice flour, water, and salt, the wrappers are rolled out, steamed, and left to dry on bamboo mats, which imprints a characteristic crosshatch pattern on them. The wrappers, about 8 inches in diameter, are ideal for spring rolls and other appetizers.

To use, they must be dipped in hot tap water for a few seconds. They can be used fresh or fried.

WONTON WRAPPERS

These are made from a dough similar to the egg roll wrappers. Indeed, egg roll wrappers can be cut into quarters to make wonton skins. Wonton skins are stuffed to make a variety of dumplings in addition to wontons. They can be filled and then boiled, pan-fried, or deep-fried.

STOCKING THE ASIAN PANTRY

I love to browse through markets in Montreal's Chinatown where the produce stands are crammed with unusual fresh vegetables. Unfamiliar fish lie stacked on ice at the fish counters, while customers stand in line at the cash registers holding grocery bags overflowing with large live crabs. In the larger grocery stores, aisle after aisle of exotic bottled and canned products tempt me. What follows is an explanation of the ingredients you will want to identify at the market and stock up on in order to make the dishes in this book.

HERBS AND VEGETABLES
Basil
Fresh Thai sweet basil, known as *horopa*, is commonly used in Thai and Vietnamese dishes. In soups and salads, it is added at the last minute for a dash of fresh flavor. *Horopa* is similar to Italian basil, which can be used as a substitute. Dried basil is never used.

Chiles, Fresh and Dried
The heat of various chiles is measured in heat units callled Scoville Units. Knowing the ratings of chiles can help you avoid unpleasant surprises. If you like your food without heat, you can always omit the chiles. If you like your food mildly spicy, jalapeños at 2,500 to 5,000 heat units are a good choice.

Among dried chiles, tiny red, green, or yellow-orange bird's-eye chiles are often used in Thai cooking; they are extremely hot at 130,000 heat units. Thai chiles are somewhat milder (but still quite hot!) at 80,000 heat units. You can make a dish hotter by including the seeds, or milder by discarding the seeds before chopping.

Note: Handle hot chiles with care, and wash your hands, cutting boards, and knives afterward.

Cilantro
Distinctively flavored fresh coriander, also called Chinese parsley, is a staple of Chinese and Southeast Asian cooking, as well as a prominent herb in Mexican cooking. The leaves look something like flat-leafed parsley, but the flavor and aroma are entirely different. Cilantro is very green and pungent, with a slight floral flavor.

Cilantro is usually sold with its roots still attached, and some recipes even call for using the whole plant—roots, stems, and all. Most recipes, however, use just the leaves. Fresh cilantro will keep in a plastic bag in the refrigerator for 4 to 5 days. It is easy to grow from seed in the garden. Do not substitute dried cilantro, which is lacking in flavor.

Daikon Radish

Also known as the "giant white radish," daikon can range from 8 to 20 inches long. It is available fresh at many health food stores. The flesh should be peeled, then sliced, julienned, or shredded. Unused portions can be stored in plastic wrap in the refrigerator for up to 2 weeks.

Garlic

There are very few recipes in this book that don't call for garlic—it's essential in Asian cooking. Often in China it is used in combination with ginger and scallions. In Thai cooking, it is combined with cilantro root and black pepper. Use only fresh garlic; do not substitute bottled minced garlic.

Ginger

Another mainstay of Asian cooking, ginger adds a fragrant, sweet spiciness to many Asian dishes, particularly in dishes from China and Japan. Ginger grows as an underground rhizome, not a root. It has a thin tan skin, which need not be peeled away if the ginger is fresh. Avoid ginger that is shriveled or soft. Look for firm, smooth rhizomes. Powdered ginger is not an acceptable substitute.

Kaffir Lime

The kaffir lime is different from the familiar Persian or Key lime. It is prized only for its intensely fragrant skin and leaves—the juice is used only in cosmetics and medicines. Kaffir lime leaves can be frozen. Rinse and pat dry with a kitchen towel. Remove the leaves from the stems. Freeze the leaves in zippered plastic bags, removing as many as needed at a time. The leaves will keep for 3 months or more. Dried leaves can be substituted for fresh. Persian or Key lime zest can replace kaffir lime zest and leaves if necessary.

Lemongrass

Also known as citronella, this intensely fragrant grass is used to add a fresh lemon flavor to dishes from Southeast Asia. Only the lower portion of the stem is used. Discard the outer leaves until you reach the more tender inner core. Whole stems can be stored in the freezer in plastic bags to be used when needed. You may also find handy-to-use minced lemongrass in the freezer section of Asian specialty food stores. One stalk of fresh lemongrass, trimmed and minced, is equivalent to 2 tablespoons frozen chopped lemongrass.

Mushrooms

I use mushrooms a lot—nothing works better with soy sauce. White button mushrooms are readily available and okay as a substitute in most recipes, but shiitakes are by far my favorite for Asian noodles. Dried shiitakes are more concentrated in flavor than fresh ones. These dried shiitakes are sometimes called "Chinese black mushrooms." The fresh shiitakes are really wonderful also. Don't use the stem of the shiitake—it is tough. Dried black fungus, also called "cloud" or "wood ear mushrooms," are thin, black, large, crinkly mushrooms that are used in stir-fries and soups. They have a delicate flavor and somewhat rubbery texture.

Sichuan Peppercorns

These look like regular peppercorns, but are actually the fruit of the prickly ash plant. They have an aromatic flavor and a slightly numbing effect on the tongue. They are also sold powdered under the Japanese name, *sansho*. You can buy the whole seeds in Chinese groceries in small plastic bags. Store them in an airtight jar in a cool, dark place for 6 to 12 months.

Star Anise

The star-shaped fruit of a Chinese evergreen, star anise lends an anise flavor to slow-cooked dishes. They can be found in Chinese groceries packed in small plastic bags. They keep for quite a long time. As long as they smell fragrant, they will add flavor.

Tamarind

Widely used in Asia for its tangy, fruity, sour flavor, tamarind is a large brown pod of a tree. It can be found fresh, dried, in cans of concentrate, or in compressed blocks of pulp with or without the seeds. The pulp is usually soaked in boiling water, then mashed and strained. The resulting purée is used in recipes.

Look for tamarind pulp in 1-pound blocks in Asian grocery stores. Store it well sealed in the refrigerator, cutting off pieces when you need them. It keeps beautifully for many months.

To Make Tamarind Purée: From a block of tamarind pulp, slice off a piece about 1/2 inch by 3 inches by 1 3/4 inches. Dip a sharp knife in boiling water and chop the pulp to a fine dice. Combine the diced pulp and 1/4 cup boiling water in a small bowl. Cover tightly and let stand for 10 to 15 minutes. Stir and mash the pulp until it combines with the water make to a purée. Press the mixture through a sieve with the back of a spoon, scraping the purée off the underside of the sieve. The tamarind purée may be refrigerated for up to 5 days, or sealed and frozen for up to 3 months. Yield: 5 tablespoons.

Note: To use tamarind concentrate, simply follow the directions on the jar for diluting the concentrate to make tamarind purée. Making your own tamarind purée from the pulp is preferable, however; the flavor is much livelier.

SAUCES, PASTES, WINES, AND VINEGARS

Bean Sauce

This brown sauce is made from fermented soy beans, often combined with garlic and spices. In the Sichuan provinces, hot bean sauce has ground chiles added to it. Hot bean sauce, sweet bean sauce, and yellow bean sauce are all types of bean sauce, but each has its own unique flavor, and they cannot be used interchangeably. Opened jars will keep indefinitely in the refrigerator.

Chili Paste with Garlic

Sold in jars and cans, chili paste (made sometimes without garlic) has ground up red chiles with vinegar, salt, and a little oil. Opened jars can be stored in the refrigerator for over a year; however, the chili paste will lose pungency over time, so adjust the amounts you use to your liking. I prefer Lan Chi brand chili paste with garlic.

Chili Sauce

Chili sauces vary from country to country. They are usually a combination of puréed red chiles and vinegar, sugar, and salt. Louisiana-style hot sauce is often an acceptable substitute. Thai chili sauces are particularly sweet; look for Sriracha brand. Szechuan brand chili sauce from Taiwan is also recommended.

Curry Paste

Both Thai and Indian curry pastes are sold in jars and cans to give cooks quick access to authentic Asian flavors. Generally curry pastes are preferable to curry powder because they offer more complex flavors and will keep indefinitely. Most are oil-based. Many include chile peppers, garlic, tamarind juice, vinegar, and different spices. Thai curry pastes come in red, green, and yellow versions, each with its own distinct flavor. Typically, Thai curry pastes are hot and contain shrimp paste, cilantro, chiles, ginger, lemongrass, and garlic. Daw Sen's from Calcutta and Patak's Mild Curry Paste are recommended, but you can make your own (see page 224). Usually a curry paste is combined with coconut milk to create an instant sauce.

Fish Sauce

Asian fish sauce is a very pungent, salty liquid that is not at all pleasant to taste in its undiluted form; but blended into a sauce, it adds a characteristic flavor to the foods of Southeast Asia in much the same way soy sauce adds a characteristic flavor to the foods of China. *Nam pla* is the Thai version and *nuoc mam* is the Vietnamese version. Both are made by layering fish and salt in huge barrels and allowing them to ferment. The resulting liquid that is poured off is the fish sauce.

Hoisin Sauce

This reddish brown sauce, both mildly spicy and sweet, is made of soy beans, vinegar, chiles, garlic, sesame, and spices. It is used to season meat and also serves as a dipping sauce. It is worth tasting several brands until you find one that you prefer—the sauces range from thick to thin, and from quite sweet to rather salty. I prefer Koon Chun brand, which is widely available. Store opened jars in the refrigerator where they will keep indefinitely. There is no substitute for this vital seasoning.

Mirin

This golden Japanese wine is too sweet to drink and so is used exclusively in cooking. It leaves a lovely glaze on grilled foods. If you can't find mirin, you can substitute a half volume of white sugar (i.e., 1/2 teaspoon sugar for each 1 teaspoon mirin).

Miso

A salty paste of fermented soy beans, miso is sold in plastic bags or tubs from the refrigerator case of many health food stores, as well as in Japanese food stores. There are several different kinds, each with its own flavor, color, and fragrance. Once opened, miso will keep for about 1 year in the refrigerator.

Oyster Sauce

A rich, mellow-tasting brown sauce made from oysters and soy sauce. It doesn't taste at all fishy and adds a rather meaty flavor to dishes in which it is used. There is no substitute for it.

Rice Wine

Chinese rice wine is used for drinking and cooking. It adds a note of sweetness to many recipes. Chinese rice wine has a sweet, smooth flavor with hints of almond. You can substitute a good-quality dry sherry for Chinese rice wine, but don't substitute Japanese sake or mirin—both are too sweet. The wine produced in Shaoxing is generally regarded as the best.

Seitan

The Chinese call it "mock meat," but it has only a remote resemblance to meat. Seitan is made from wheat gluten. It has a firm, chewy texture and a bland flavor. Although you can find seitan in canned form, I prefer fresh seitan in plastic packs sold in the refrigerator section of most health food stores. The Japanese call it "FU." It is sold fresh or dried in specialty food stores.

Soy Sauce

Made from a fermentation of cooked soybeans and wheat, soy sauce is essential in many Asian noodle dishes. If you look at the shelves of almost any grocery store in any Chinatown, you are likely to be confused by the profusion of soy sauces—thin soy sauce, black soy sauce, mushroom soy, etc. For most recipes, regular ("thin") soy sauce is just fine—Kikkoman, a very good brand, is widely available. Mushroom soy sauce is a little sweeter and richer in flavor; lovely to have on hand and good on stir fries, but regular soy sauce can be used instead. Do avoid the American-made, supermarket brand soy sauces made with hydrolyzed vegetable protein, corn syrup, and caramel coloring. They just won't produce authentically flavored dishes.

Toasted Sesame Oil

Dark sesame oil, made from toasted sesame seeds (as opposed to light-colored, cold-pressed sesame oil made from raw seeds), is used as a flavoring in Chinese and Japanese cooking. It adds a strong nutty flavor, color, aroma, and shine to noodle dishes. It is available almost everywhere. There is no substitute for it.

Vinegar

White distilled vinegar offers a sharp, uncomplicated sour flavoring and is used in many dipping sauces. Rice vinegar on the other hand is widely used for its mellow, light flavor. Japanese brands tend to be smoother in flavor than Chinese brands. Chinese black vinegar, with a faintly sweet flavor, is also distilled from rice and is used for seasoning in Chinese dishes. Balsamic vinegar makes an acceptable substitute.

MISCELLANEOUS ITEMS
Bonito Flakes, Dried
Shaved flakes of dried bonito, a fish that is variously described as a type of tuna, mackerel, or intermediate fish between tuna and mackerel, is an essential ingredient of dashi, a traditional Japanese stock. The shaved bonito looks like very fine wood shavings. Buy it in plastic bags; if it is stored in an airtight bag or container, it will keep indefinitely.

Coconut Milk
Canned coconut milk, usually from Thailand, is readily available in most supermarkets. It is unsweetened. Coconut cream on the other hand is sweetened and is used in mixed drinks. Canned coconut milk generally has a nearly solid layer at the top, with a thinner liquid below. Shake vigorously before opening the can and whisk as needed to mix the two layers completely.

In a pinch, you can make coconut milk from dried, shredded, unsweetened coconut. Combine 1/2 cup of dried shredded coconut with 1 1/2 cups boiling water and set aside to cool to room temperature. Transfer to a blender and purée. Line a fine mesh strainer with cheesecloth and strain the mixture through the cheesecloth, pressing on the coconut solids with the back of a spoon to release all of the liquid. You should have about 1 1/4 cups coconut milk.

Kombu
Of the many types of seaweed sold wherever Japanese foods are available, kombu, or *konbu* as it is sometimes spelled, is a type of kelp that is used to flavor dashi broth. It has a deep olive-green, almost black, color and a strong briny aroma. It is usually sold dried, cut into 12-inch lengths. The seaweed sometimes develops a harmless white mold on its surface, which is why some recipes call for wiping off the kombu with a damp cloth before using. Because kombu has such an intense flavor, it can be used twice before it loses flavor.

Tofu

The Chinese call it "bean curd," the Japanese "tofu," but it is all the same product—a protein-rich "cheese" made from soy milk. The tofu I buy is "firm" and stands up to a stir-fry without crumbling, as opposed to the Japanese-style "silken" tofu, which has a custard-smooth texture and a tendency to fall apart. I buy mine in bulk from a health food store, meaning I buy cakes of bean curd from a large bucket in which the tofu floats in water. When I get home, I transfer the tofu to a clean plastic container and store it in fresh water. If the water is changed daily, the tofu will stay fresh for 7 to 10 days.

If you have any doubts about the freshness of bulk tofu, or the sanitation practices in the store, you may be happier buying yours in the sealed plastic tubs available in most supermarkets. For stir-fries, buy extra-firm or firm tofu. Seasoned tofu or smoked tofu, found in health food stores, is handy to add flavor to quick stir-fries.

Sometimes a recipe calls for draining off the extra moisture in the tofu. To do so, wrap the tofu in a clean cotton kitchen towel. Place a heavy weight on top of the tofu (a cutting board weighted down with a juice can works fine) and set aside for about 30 minutes.

A FEW COOKING TIPS AND SERVING SUGGESTIONS

The key to a good stir-fry is high heat. Which pan to use depends, in part, on how hot you can get your pan. The metal ring which enables a wok to sit on an electric burner raises the wok too far above the burner to allow for effective heat transfer. So if you are cooking on an electric burner, you will get better results using a skillet rather than a wok. If you are cooking on a gas stove, however, the wok can sit directly on the burner, so the wok is the better choice.

Several recipes specify holding cooked noodles in a 200°F oven to keep them warm. An alternative is to reheat the noodles at the last minute. There are several ways you can do this.

To Rewarm Cooked Noodles: Place the noodles in a microwave-safe container, cover, and heat on high for 1 minute. Check the temperature of the noodles. A large dish of noodles may require an additional 30 seconds. Or, to rewarm the noodles Asian-style, using a wire-mesh strainer, dip a single portion of noodles into boiling water, drain, then place in individual serving bowls. If you have a large mesh basket, you can dip more than one portion at a time.

Most of the recipes serve 4 as a main course. If you are serving an

Asian-style meal with several dishes, figure that a dish that serves 4 as a main course will serve 6 to 8 people when served with other dishes in a multidish meal.

Eating long noodles in Asia symbolizes a wish for a long life. While I don't wish my life to be shortened, I do find shorter noodles easier to eat. Many of the recipes specify cutting the noodles into shorter lengths with a pair of kitchen scissors. This step is optional for those who are comfortable slurping long noodles—which is best done from a bowl held close to the lips.

All Wrapped Up

Vietnamese Fresh Spring Rolls

You may ask why I included spring rolls and egg rolls in a noodle book. It took me a while and then I understood what hadn't been obvious to me at first: the wraps are noodles.

Fresh spring rolls—ones that aren't fried—are always a revelation to those who meet them for the first time. These rice paper rolls, filled with fresh greens, shrimp, and noodles, couldn't be more colorful.

12 medium raw shrimp in the shell (5 to 6 ounces)

4 ounces dried rice vermicelli

1 medium carrot, shredded

1/2 teaspoon sugar

About 8 round rice papers (8 1/2 inches in diameter)

1 small head Boston or red leaf lettuce, leaves separated

2 red serrano chiles, seeded and julienned (optional)

2 cups bean sprouts

1/2 cup basil leaves (Thai holy basil or sweet basil)

Chives (optional)

1/2 cup cilantro leaves

Dipping Sauce

1/4 cup shredded carrot

1/4 cup shredded daikon

1 teaspoon sugar

1/2 cup Nuoc Cham (page 208)

1 Bring a medium-size pot of water to a boil. Turn off the heat and add the shrimp.

2 Cover and let the shrimp poach for 3 minutes. Drain, plunge into cold water, drain again, and peel. Slice the shrimp in half lengthwise.

3 Cook the noodles in a medium-size pot of boiling water until just done, about 3 to 5 minutes. Drain, rinse under cold water, and drain again. Scissor into 3-inch lengths.

4 In a small bowl, combine the shredded carrot with the sugar for 10 minutes to soften.

5 To assemble the spring rolls, lay out all the ingredients in the order needed. First the rice papers, with a bowl of warm water and a damp cloth, then the fresh ingredients: lettuce, rice vermicelli, carrots, chiles, if using, bean sprouts, basil leaves, chives, if using, shrimp, and cilantro.

6 Dip a rice paper into the warm water, lay it on a kitchen towel. Lay a piece of lettuce on the bottom third of the paper. Place a tablespoon or two of rice vermicelli along the lettuce, then a layer of carrots and a few slivers of red chile, pressing the ingredients gently together as you work. Next, lay a thin layer of bean sprouts and a few basil leaves. Pressing the ingredients together, make one roll of the cylinder and fold each side of the wrapper in, over the filling. Lay 2 or 3 chives on the roll, with an inch extending over the end, then 2 or 3 shrimp halves, cut side down. Place 2 or 3 large cilantro leaves on the shrimp and roll into a tight cylinder with the chives extending out from one end. Place the rolls on a platter and cover with a damp towel to stay moist. They may be stored at room temperature for a few hours. Do not refrigerate, as the rice paper toughens in cold temperatures.

7 To make the dipping sauce, combine the shredded carrot and daikon in a small bowl with the sugar to soften for 10 to 15 minutes. Stir in the Nuoc Cham.

8 To serve, cut the rolls into 2 or 3 pieces and stand upright on a small plate with a bowl of the dipping sauce on the side.

NOTE: Rice paper wrappers, thin translucent sheets that take on the pattern of the woven bamboo trays on which they dry, are found wherever Vietnamese foods are sold under the name *banh trang*. Rice paper is a little difficult to work with the first time around. In their dry state, they are quite brittle and must be handled carefully. To soften, dip the sheets in warm water just long enough to make them flexible. With a little practice you will discover just how much softening the wrappers require to be flexible without disintegrating in your hands. Expect that some will break before softening. Some will also tear as you fill them and have to be discarded.

Southeast Asian Spring Rolls

YIELD: 6 FIRST-COURSE SERVINGS

Spring rolls—deep-fried rolls filled with fresh ingredients—are tasty morsels found throughout Asia. In Vietnam and Thailand, the filling might include chewy cellophane noodles, as well as pork and fresh vegetables. These are especially lovely served Vietnamese style—on a platter of fresh greens and herbs. The leaves are used to wrap around the spring rolls, which are then dipped in a sweet and sour sauce.

1 (1.75-ounce) skein cellophane noodles

2 tablespoons peanut oil or canola oil

1-inch cube fresh ginger, minced

3 garlic cloves, minced

1/2 pound ground pork

8 cups finely shredded green cabbage

2 carrots, finely shredded

3 scallions, including some green parts, chopped

1 tablespoon chopped fresh cilantro

2 tablespoons Asian fish sauce

Oil for deep-frying

Cornstarch

12 spring roll or lumpia wrappers

Paste made from 1 tablespoon each of flour and water, or 1 egg white, beaten

Southeast Asian Sweet and Sour Sauce (page 209) or Nuoc Cham (page 208).

1 Cover the cellophane noodles with hot tap water and set aside to soften for about 15 minutes. Drain in a colander, rinse in cold water, and drain well. Scissor into 3-inch pieces.

2 Heat the oil in a large skillet or wok. Add the ginger, garlic, and pork, and stir-fry, breaking up the pork with the spoon, just until the pork loses its pink color, about 4 minutes. Remove from the

skillet with a slotted spoon and add to the cellophane noodles in the colander. Squeeze out any excess moisture.

3 Add the cabbage to the skillet and stir-fry until limp, about 2 minutes. Add to the colander and allow to drain for a few minutes.

4 In a large bowl, combine the cellophane noodles, pork, cabbage, carrots, scallions, cilantro, and fish sauce. Mix well.

5 Begin preheating the oil to 375°F.

6 Lightly dust your work surface and a plate with cornstarch. Place a wrapper with one corner (if the wrapper is square) toward you on the prepared work surface. Keep the open package of wrappers covered with a damp towel. Place about 2 heaping tablespoons of filling just below the center of the wrapper. Fold the bottom of the wrapper up over the filling, coaxing the filling into a log shape. Fold in the sides, then roll up the spring roll, tucking in the sides as you go. Seal the last corner with a paste of flour and water or beaten egg white. Place seam side down on a plate.

7 When the oil is hot, fry the spring rolls, no more than three at a time, for 2 to 3 minutes, or until golden brown, turning them so they brown evenly. Remove from the oil with a slotted spoon and stand on end in a colander to drain for a few minutes before serving.

8 Serve hot, with the Southeast Asian Sweet and Sour Sauce or Nuoc Cham.

NOTE: Be sure to buy spring roll or lumpia wrappers, which are much thinner than the American-style egg roll wrapper. Rice paper wrappers will do as a substitute.

Vegetarian Pot Stickers

YIELD: 6 FIRST-COURSE SERVINGS

Pot stickers received their name because one side invariably sticks to the pot when they are fried and then steamed in the same skillet. You can avoid the problem by boiling them first, then frying, which is what I usually do. For the traditionalists, I've also included a pan-fry method using a nonstick skillet (see note below).

1/2 teaspoon peanut oil

1/2 teaspoon toasted sesame oil

1/2 teaspoon minced garlic

1/2 teaspoon minced ginger

2 scallions, minced

2 tablespoons minced carrot

2 tablespoons finely chopped onion

1/2 cup tightly packed tofu (3 1/2 ounces or 1 cube measuring 2 by 2 by 1 3/4 inches)

1/4 cup finely chopped bok choy

1/4 cup chopped fresh bean sprouts

1 tablespoon mushroom soy sauce, tamari, or soy sauce

Freshly ground black pepper

30 round dumpling wrappers

1 egg, beaten

Peanut oil for frying

Soy Ginger Dipping Sauce (page 206), Nuoc Cham (page 208), or Toasted Sesame Sauce (page 212)

1   In a small skillet, heat the peanut oil and sesame oil over medium heat until hot. Add the garlic, ginger, scallions, carrot, and onion. Stir-fry for about 3 minutes, until the onion begins to soften but not brown. Remove to a medium-size bowl. Add the tofu, crumbling it with a fork against the sides of the bowl. Add the bok choy, bean sprouts, soy sauce, and black pepper to taste.

28

2 To fill the wrappers, place a teaspoon of filling off center on the wrapper. Brush the edge of half the wrapper with beaten egg and fold it in half, sealing it tight with your fingers. Keep the dumplings covered with plastic wrap to prevent drying out. Refrigerate until cooking and plan to do this within 5 hours.

3 *To cook the dumplings the nonstick way:* Bring 4 quarts of water to a simmer. Add about half the dumplings to the pot, quickly one by one. Keeping the water at a simmer, cook for about 5 minutes until just tender. Remove the dumplings carefully with a large flat strainer and drain. Repeat with the remaining dumplings. Heat 2 tablespoons peanut oil in a large nonstick skillet over high heat. Carefully set the dumplings in the pan and fry on one side only for 2 to 3 minutes, until lightly browned.

4 Serve hot with the Soy Ginger Dipping Sauce, Nuoc Cham, or Toasted Sesame Sauce for dipping.

NOTE: To cook the dumplings *by the traditional pan-fry method:* Heat 3 tablespoons of water and 1 tablespoon of peanut oil in a large nonstick skillet and fry the dumplings, covered, over high heat until the water has evaporated and the dumplings are cooked. Test one, and if they are not quite done, add a little water and simmer, covered, for a few more minutes.

Steamed Shrimp Shao Mai

YIELD: ABOUT 6 FIRST-COURSE SERVINGS

Shao mai are always a favorite at dim sum, but at home most people serve dumplings as a first course. For a special evening of Pacific Rim flavors, serve 3 or 4 dumplings per person in a pool of green Basil Lemongrass Sauce (page 216). A food processor does a good job on all the mincing this recipe requires; dry the shrimp on paper towels before placing in the food processor.

3/4 pound raw shrimp, shelled, deveined, and minced

2 scallions, white and green parts, minced

1/3 cup water chestnuts or jicama, minced

1 teaspoon minced garlic

1 teaspoon minced ginger

2 teaspoons toasted sesame oil

1 tablespoon oyster sauce

1 1/2 teaspoons mirin or 3/4 teaspoon sugar

Freshly ground black or white pepper

30 round wonton wrappers

Garnish: Carrot shavings and snow pea shoots (optional)

Basil Lemongrass Sauce (page 216), Nuoc Cham (page 208), or Soy Ginger Dipping Sauce (page 206)

1 To make the filling, combine the shrimp, scallions, water chestnuts, garlic, ginger, sesame oil, oyster sauce, mirin, and a dash of pepper. Mix well.

2 Place a rounded teaspoon of the shrimp mixture in the center of a wonton wrapper and bring the sides up around the filling. Squeeze the dumpling in a ring part way up the side, making a "waist" with a ruffle above. Tap the bottom on a flat work surface to ensure that it can stand upright. The top of the dumpling should be open, showing the filling in the center. Insert a shaving of peeled carrot and a tiny sprig of snow pea shoot in the center, if you wish.

3 Place the dumplings in a steamer with 1/2 inch or more space between them. Steam, covered, over boiling water for about 7 or 8 minutes, until cooked through. Serve warm with Basil Lemongrass Sauce, Nuoc Cham, or Soy Ginger Dipping Sauce.

NOTE: These are best if you can steam and serve them immediately after making them—but that is rarely practical. To hold them for a few hours, place the formed dumplings on baking sheets that have been covered with parchment paper. Cover well with plastic wrap and refrigerate. Bring to room temperature before steaming.

Ginger-Chicken Pot Stickers

YIELD: ABOUT 8 FIRST-COURSE SERVINGS

These spicy dumplings can be simmered first in hot water and then briefly pan-fried on one side, or (the traditional way) pan-fried fast and then steamed in the same pan. Either way results in a tender crisp dumpling. A shallow bowl of warm dumplings drizzled with a light cashew sauce provides pure comfort.

1 1/2 cups chopped bok choy

3/4 teaspoon salt

1 tablespoon peanut oil

1 teaspoon toasted sesame oil

1/2 teaspoon Hot Chili Oil (page 223)

1 tablespoon minced garlic

1 teaspoon minced fresh ginger

1/2 pound finely chopped chicken breast

1/4 cup chopped scallions, including some green parts

2 tablespoons chopped cilantro leaves and stems

1 tablespoon oyster sauce

1 tablespoon soy sauce

Freshly ground black pepper

About 48 round wonton wrappers

1 egg, beaten

Peanut oil for frying

Cashew Sauce (page 213), Soy Ginger Dipping Sauce (page 206), or Toasted Sesame Sauce (page 212)

1   Place the bok choy in a large flat dish and sprinkle with the salt. Let stand for 15 minutes, stirring once in a while with a fork. Then squeeze handfuls of the bok choy to remove as much water as possible.

2   In a large skillet or wok, heat the peanut, sesame, and hot chili oil over medium heat. Add the garlic, ginger, chicken, and bok choy

and sauté for 2 or 3 minutes until no pink remains on the chicken breast. Remove from the heat and add the scallions, cilantro, oyster sauce, soy sauce, and pepper to taste.

3 To fill the wrappers, place a teaspoon of filling off center on the wrapper. Brush the edge of half the wrapper with beaten egg and fold it in half, sealing it tight with your fingers. Keep the dumplings covered with plastic wrap to prevent drying out. Refrigerate until cooking and plan to do this within 5 hours.

4 *To cook the dumplings the nonstick way:* Bring 4 quarts of water to a simmer. Add about a dozen of the dumplings to the pot quickly, one by one. Keeping the water at a simmer, cook for about 5 minutes until just tender. Remove the dumplings carefully with a large flat strainer and drain. Repeat with the remaining dumplings. Heat 2 tablespoons peanut oil in a large nonstick skillet over high heat. Carefully set the dumplings in the pan—do not crowd the pan—and fry on one side only for 2 to 3 minutes, until lightly browned. Set aside and keep warm. Repeat with the remaining dumplings.

5 Serve hot with Cashew Sauce, Soy Ginger Dipping Sauce, or Toasted Sesame Sauce.

NOTE: To cook dumplings *by the traditional pan-fry method* (you may have to do this in 2 or 3 batches): Heat 3 tablespoons of water and 1 tablespoon of peanut oil in a large nonstick skillet and fry the dumplings, covered, over high heat until the water has evaporated and the dumplings are cooked. Test one, and if they are not quite done, add a little water and simmer, covered, for a few more minutes. Set aside and keep warm while you cook the remaining dumplings.

Lemongrass Pork Dumplings

YIELD: 6 FIRST-COURSE SERVINGS

*These delicately seasoned dumplings can be served in a couple of differ-
ent ways. Try two or three of these dumplings in Lemony Chicken Broth
(page 221) garnished with thin slices of fresh red chile as a first course.
Or serve them as a side dish to accompany the Green Soba Salad with
snow pea shoots for a flavorful light meal. Or serve them as an appe-
tizer, with Nuoc Cham (page 208), adding some shredded carrot and
daikon to the dipping sauce. Any way you serve them, you'll be happy
you've captured the elusive, delicate flavor of lemongrass.*

1/2 pound lean ground pork

1 stalk lemongrass (bottom 6 inches), finely chopped, or 2
tablespoons frozen chopped lemongrass

1/4 cup chopped scallions, including some green parts

1 tablespoon chopped garlic

2 tablespoons chopped fresh basil

1/2 teaspoon cornstarch

1 tablespoon oyster sauce

1 tablespoon soy sauce

1 egg white

Freshly ground black pepper

30 round wonton wrappers

1 egg, beaten

Nuoc Cham (page 208) or Soy Lime Dipping Sauce
(page 207)

1 In a small bowl, combine the pork, lemongrass, scallions, garlic,
and basil. In another small bowl, combine the cornstarch, oyster
sauce, and soy sauce and add to the pork mixture. Slightly whip
the egg white and stir into the pork. Season with pepper.

2 To fill the wrappers, place 2 teaspoons of the filling off center on
the wrapper. Brush the edge of half the wrapper with beaten egg,
and fold in half, sealing tight with your fingers. Keep the

dumplings covered with plastic wrap to prevent drying out. Refrigerate for up to 5 hours before cooking.

3 To cook the dumplings, bring 4 quarts of water to a simmer. Add about a dozen dumplings to the pot quickly, one by one, keeping the water at a simmer (not boiling). Cook the dumplings about 5 minutes, until just tender. Remove them carefully with a flat Chinese strainer and drain. Repeat with the remaining dumplings. Serve hot with Nuoc Cham or Soy Lime Dipping Sauce.

Tamarind Pork Wontons

YIELD: ABOUT 8 FIRST-COURSE SERVINGS

The tamarind ginger combination is tart and delicious, blending well with the pork.

2 tablespoons minced fresh ginger

1/4 cup tamarind purée (see pages 16-17)

1 tablespoon mirin

2 teaspoons sugar

1/4 cup minced scallions

2/3 cup chopped water chestnuts

1 teaspoon Hot Chili Oil (page 223)

1/4 teaspoon freshly ground pepper

1/2 teaspoon salt

1 pound coarsely ground pork

About 45 (3-inch) square wonton skins

1 egg, beaten

Corn or peanut oil for frying

Soy Ginger Dipping Sauce (page 206), Ginger Apricot Sauce, (page 210), or Toasted Sesame Sauce (page 212)

1   In a small bowl, combine the ginger, tamarind, mirin, and sugar. Cover, and microwave on high until the mixture boils, about 85 seconds. Remove and keep covered. Set aside for 5 minutes.

2   Combine the scallions, water chestnuts, hot chili oil, pepper, and salt. Add the ground pork and stir to mix. Add the tamarind mixture and combine well. (At this point, the filling may be refrigerated for several hours, or overnight. Place plastic wrap directly on top of the filling to seal out any air.)

3   Make the wontons by placing a heaping teaspoon of filling just above the center of the wrapper. Moisten the edges of the wrapper with beaten egg and fold into a triangle, pressing carefully to expel any air. Bring the 2 side points together and seal with beaten egg,

pinching the ends to form a little cap. Keep the finished wontons covered lightly to stay moist.

4 The wontons may be refrigerated for a few hours, or overnight, covered with plastic wrap. Fry them directly from the refrigerator to keep the wrappers from becoming soggy.

5 Heat about 2 inches of oil in a wok or deep skillet over high heat to 375°F. Fry a few wontons at a time, adjusting the heat to maintain a steady temperature. Fry to a light golden brown, about 1 1/2 to 2 minutes. Remove with a mesh strainer and drain on paper towels laid out on a paper bag. Hold in a 200°F oven until you are ready to serve.

6 Serve with Soy Ginger Dipping Sauce, Ginger Apricot Sauce, or Toasted Sesame Sauce.

NOTE: These crunchy morsels need to be kept hot to stay crisp.

Ginger-Pork Shao Mai
YIELD: ABOUT 8 FIRST-COURSE SERVINGS

These little gingery pork dumplings have been a favorite in my family for many years. The ginger preserves add a pleasant sweetness to the flavors of the toasted sesame oil and hoisin sauce.

1 pound pork, coarsely ground or minced

1/2 cup water chestnuts or jicama, minced

3 scallions, white and green parts, minced

2 tablespoons ginger preserves or 1 tablespoon minced fresh ginger

1 1/2 tablespoons hoisin sauce

2 teaspoons toasted sesame oil

Freshly ground black pepper

40 round wonton wrappers

Ginger Apricot Sauce (page 210) or Soy Lime Dipping Sauce (page 207)

1   In a medium-size bowl, combine the pork, water chestnuts or jicama, scallions, ginger preserves or ginger, hoisin sauce, sesame oil, and a small amount of black pepper. Mix well.

2   Place a rounded teaspoon of the pork mixture in the center of a wonton wrapper and bring the sides up around the filling. Squeeze the dumpling in a ring part way up the side, making a "waist" with a ruffle above. Tap the bottom on a flat work surface to ensure that it can stand upright. The top of the dumpling should be open, showing the filling in the center.

3   Place the shao mai in a steamer with 1/2 inch or more of space between them. Steam, covered, over boiling water for about 7 or 8 minutes, until cooked through. Serve warm with Ginger Apricot Sauce or Soy Lime Dipping Sauce.

Cool Salads

Summer Vegetable Salad
with Cellophane Noodles

YIELD: 4 MAIN-COURSE SERVINGS

These slippery cellophane noodles with fresh vegetables have a sharp vinegary dressing, perfect for hot weather. A bonus here: this salad is fat-free.

6 (1.75-ounce) skeins cellophane noodles

1 English cucumber, halved and thinly sliced

3 large carrots, coarsely grated (approximately 2 1/4 cups)

3/4 cup julienned red bell pepper

6 ounces snow peas, julienned

6 scallions, sliced thin diagonally

Garnish: Cilantro sprigs

Dressing

6 tablespoons Asian fish sauce

6 tablespoons rice vinegar

1 tablespoon minced garlic

3 tablespoons fresh lime juice

3 tablespoons mirin or 1 1/2 tablespoons sugar

1/4 cup chopped fresh cilantro

1 Cover the cellophane noodles with hot tap water and set aside to soften for 15 minutes. Drain in a colander, rinse in cold water, and drain well. Scissor the noodles into 4-inch lengths.

2 For the dressing, combine the fish sauce, rice vinegar, garlic, lime juice, mirin, and cilantro and mix well.

3 In a large salad bowl, combine the noodles with the cucumber, carrots, red bell pepper, snow peas, and scallions. Toss the salad with the dressing. Garnish with cilantro and serve.

Cold Spicy Cucumber Noodles

YIELD: 4 TO 6 SIDE-DISH SERVINGS

Sweet potato starch noodles haven't attracted as big a following in the U.S. as wheat and rice flour noodles. Here's a recipe that can be made with noodles made from mung beans (cellophane noodles) or sweet potato starch. Both are delicate, translucent noodles that absorb flavors from other ingredients.

3 (1.75-ounce) skeins cellophane (mung bean starch) noodles or 6 ounces sweet potato starch glass vermicelli

2 teaspoons chili paste with garlic

3 tablespoons Chinese black vinegar or balsamic vinegar

2 tablespoons soy sauce

1 tablespoon light brown sugar

1 tablespoon peanut oil

3/4 pound English cucumbers, halved and sliced 1/4-inch thick

3 fresh jalapeño, serrano, or Thai bird chiles

2 tablespoons roasted unsalted peanuts, crushed or chopped (optional)

1   *If using cellophane noodles,* cover the noodles with hot tap water and set aside to soften for 15 minutes. *If using sweet potato starch glass vermicelli,* cover the noodles with boiling water and set aside to soften for 10 minutes. Drain the noodles in a colander, rinse in cold water, then leave to drain in the colander for 2 or 3 minutes. Scissor into 3-inch lengths.

2   In a medium bowl, combine the chili paste, vinegar, soy sauce, brown sugar, and oil. Stir to dissolve the sugar. Add the noodles, cucumbers, and chiles and toss to combine. Chill for an hour before serving. Just before serving, garnish with a sprinkling of crushed peanuts, if desired, if desired.

NOTE: How spicy this dish is depends very much on your choice of chiles. The choices here are listed from mild to hot, with Thai bird chiles being among the hottest chiles in the world.

Chilled Somen Salad
with Sesame Dressing

For hot-weather dining, nothing is more appealing than a chilled noodle salad from Japan. In this recipe, each diner is given a bowl of noodles chilled with ice cubes, then everyone chooses their own garnishes. The contrasting flavors and textures, along with the piquant sesame dressing, is guaranteed to perk up any heat-wilted spirits.

Sesame Dressing

2 tablespoons toasted sesame seeds

2 teaspoons toasted sesame oil

3 tablespoons soy sauce

3 tablespoons rice vinegar

2 teaspoons mirin or 1 teaspoon sugar

1/4 pound thin asparagus, trimmed

8 shiitake mushrooms, stems discarded

8 ounces somen noodles

3 large scallions, finely julienned

1/4 cup finely sliced shiso or basil leaves

1/2 cup grated carrot (1 medium carrot)

3 tablespoons grated fresh ginger

1 (5.5-ounce) package marinated tofu, cut in 3/4-inch squares (optional)

1   To make the dressing, crush the sesame seeds or grind in a mini food processor. Add the sesame oil, soy sauce, rice vinegar, and mirin and mix well. Set aside.

2   In a medium-size pot of boiling water, blanch the asparagus for 1 minute. Plunge into cold water briefly, then drain. Blanch the shiitakes in the boiling water for 20 seconds, plunge into cold water, and drain. Slice the asparagus diagonally into 2-inch pieces and slice the shiitake caps in 1/4-inch slices. In a small bowl, toss the sliced shiitakes with 2 teaspoons of the sesame dressing.

3 Cook the somen noodles in a large pot of boiling water until just done, about 5 minutes. Drain and rinse under cold water. Drain again. Or, cook the noodles by the Japanese *sashimizu* method: Bring a large pot of water to a boil. Add the noodles and stir. When the water returns to a boil, add 1 cup cold water. Again, when the water returns to a boil, add 1 cup cold water. Taste a noodle. It should cook to a tender firmness shortly. Drain and rinse with cold water. Drain again.

4 Divide the noodles among the serving bowls and place a few ice cubes in each bowl. Present the chilled asparagus, shiitakes, scallions, shiso or basil leaves, carrot, ginger, and tofu, if using, in attractive bowls in the center of the table. Serve the sesame dressing in individual small serving bowls.

NOTE: Shiso leaves are frequently used as garnishes in Japan. The tangy, attractive leaves of *Perilla frutescens* (beefsteak plant) are related to mint. Basil isn't really a substitute for the flavor, but it works here.

Cold Soba Noodles
and **Vegetables**

YIELD: 4 TO 6 MAIN-COURSE SERVINGS

These cold, chewy buckwheat noodles with crisp vegetables and a sweet, salty, and sour dressing have a lovely balance of flavors and texture. It is somewhat of a misnomer to call the liquid portion of this salad a "dressing." Consider it, instead, a delightful chilled broth that can be drunk from the bowl when the noodles are gone. This is wonderful made ahead and served icy cold in bowls. If you do so, refrigerate the noodles, vegetables, and broth in separate, well-covered containers.

12 ounces soba noodles, fresh or dried

1 medium-size daikon radish, grated

1 carrot, peeled and grated

1/2 cup snow pea shoots

4 scallions, thinly sliced

2 tablespoons rice wine vinegar

1 tablespoon mirin

1 teaspoon sugar

1/2 teaspoon salt

Garnish: 1 tablespoon toasted sesame seeds

Cold Broth Dressing

1 1/2 cups Dashi (page 215 or made from dashi concentrate)

4 tablespoons mirin

2 teaspoons peeled, grated ginger

2 scallions, finely chopped

1 Cook the soba noodles in 3 quarts of boiling water until just tender, about 5 to 7 minutes. Drain and rinse thoroughly to cool. Or use the *sashimizu* method: Bring a large pot of water to a boil. Add the noodles and cook for 2 minutes. Add 1 cup of cold water and return to a boil. Repeat the process twice. Simmer the noodles until tender, about 5 minutes. Drain and rinse in cold water, rubbing the noodles together to remove the surface starch.

2 Combine the daikon, carrot, snow pea shoots, and scallions in a bowl. Add the vinegar, mirin, sugar, and salt and mix well.

3 Combine all the broth ingredients in a separate bowl.

4 To serve, divide the noodles among the bowls. Arrange the vegetables over the noodles and pour the broth over all. Garnish with the toasted sesame seeds.

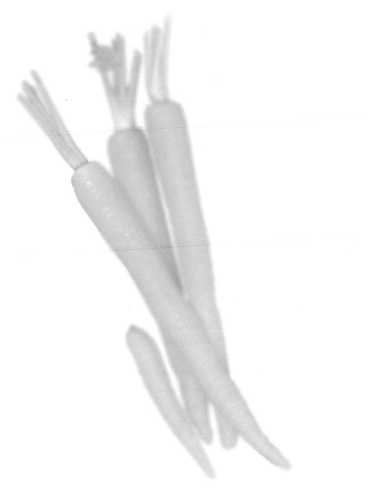

Cold Seafood
with Glass Noodles
YIELD: 4 MAIN-COURSE SERVINGS

The fat sweet potato starch glass noodles are definitely the choice noodles here. Being big and slippery, they slurp up flavorings. They are a particularly good accompaniment to seafood.

Noodles

8 ounces sweet potato starch glass vermicellli or
4 (1.75-ounce) skeins cellophane noodles

2 teaspoons toasted sesame oil

1 tablespoon soy sauce

Dressing

1 1/2 tablespoons finely minced lemongrass

1 teaspoon minced garlic

1/4 cup sliced scallions

1 tablespoon minced fresh red serrano chiles

3 tablespoons lime juice

1 tablespoon rice vinegar

1 teaspoon sugar

2 tablespoons Asian fish sauce

1 1/2 tablespoons peanut or canola oil

Seafood

2 tablespoons peanut or canola oil

1/2 pound firm-fleshed fish, such as salmon, red snapper, swordfish, or tuna, skin removed, flesh cut into 1/2-inch slices across the grain, and slices halved

1/2 pound large shrimp, peeled and deveined

1/3 pound sea scallops, halved across the grain

3 cups shredded lettuce and herbs or mesclun

Freshly ground white or black pepper

Garnish: Lime wedges and/or chile pepper flower
(see Note)

1   *If using cellophane noodles,* cover the noodles with hot tap water and set aside for 15 minutes to soften. *If using sweet potato starch vermicelli,* cover the noodles with boiling water and set aside to soften for 10 minutes. Drain the noodles in a colander, rinse in cold water, then leave to drain in the colander for 2 or 3 minutes. Scissor into 3-inch lengths.

2   In a small bowl, combine the sesame oil and soy sauce and pour over the glass noodles. Toss, cover well, and refrigerate.

3   In a small bowl, combine the dressing ingredients. Cover and refrigerate.

4   Heat 1 tablespoon of the peanut or canola oil in a nonstick skillet over high heat until hot but not smoking. Sauté the fish for about 2 or 3 minutes a side, until just cooked. Remove to a plate. Add the remaining 1 tablespoon peanut oil and sauté the shrimp for about 30 seconds a side, just until pink. Remove to a plate. Sauté the scallops, briefly, about a minute on each side and remove to a plate.

5   To serve, arrange a layer of lettuce or greens on a large serving dish. Arrange a layer of noodles over the greens, then a layer of seafood over the noodles. Grind fresh pepper and pour the dressing over the seafood. Toss the salad. Garnish with lime wedges or a chile pepper flower.

NOTE: To make a chile pepper flower, slice a chile from the tip most of the way to the stem a few times. Remove the center core and place the chile in ice water for an hour or two.

Vietnamese Rice Noodle Salad
with Shrimp

This classic light Vietnamese salad makes a delightful summer meal. It can be made well ahead of time and is oil-free. If you wish to save time, purchase precooked, peeled shrimp.

1 pound dried thin (1/8-inch) rice sticks or rice vermicelli

1 pound medium shrimp, peeled and deveined

1/2 lime

1 carrot, julienned

1 cucumber, peeled, seeded, and cut into thin strips

1 scallion, including green part, sliced

1/2 cup cilantro leaves

1/2 cup mint leaves

1 cup watercress sprigs

Garnish: 2 to 3 tablespoons chopped roasted peanuts

Dressing

2/3 cup Asian fish sauce

1/2 cup white vinegar

1/3 cup sugar

2 garlic cloves, minced

1 Cook the rice noodles in a large pot of boiling water until just done, about 3 to 5 minutes. Drain and rinse well with cold water.

2 For the dressing, combine the fish sauce, vinegar, sugar, and the garlic in a small saucepan. Heat gently, stirring constantly, until the sugar is dissolved. Set aside to cool.

3 Add the shrimp and lime to a medium-size pot of boiling water and poach the shrimp in barely simmering water until pink and firm, about 1 to 3 minutes. Drain, discard the lime, and set aside.

4 Place the vermicelli in a large serving bowl and pour half of the

dressing over it. Toss well. Add the shrimp, carrot, cucumber, and scallion and toss again.

5 Make a bed of the cilantro, mint, and watercress greens on individual plates. Divide the salad among them and garnish with the chopped peanuts. Serve at once, passing the remaining dressing at the table.

Vietnamese Grilled Shrimp and Rice Noodle Salad

YIELD: 4 MAIN-COURSE SERVINGS

A variation on the theme of the previous recipe, the shrimp here is grilled rather than poached. I enjoyed this wonderful salad in a Vietnamese restaurant in Montreal. It was also delicious made with skewers of chicken instead of shrimp.

1 pound shrimp, peeled and deveined

1 tablespoon minced fresh lemongrass or grated lemon zest

1 teaspoon minced fresh ginger

2 teaspoons Asian fish sauce

1 tablespoon vegetable oil

6 to 8 ounces dried rice vermicelli

2 to 3 cups shredded red or green leaf or romaine lettuce

2 cups fresh mung bean sprouts

1/3 cup roughly chopped Thai or sweet basil leaves

1/3 cup roughly chopped mint leaves

1/3 cup roughly chopped cilantro leaves (optional)

2 to 3 tablespoons crushed roasted unsalted peanuts

Garnish: Cilantro or basil sprigs

1 cup Nuoc Cham (page 208) or Chili Dipping Sauce (page 211)

1 In a small bowl, combine the shrimp with the lemongrass, ginger, fish sauce, and vegetable oil. Cover and set aside for 20 minutes or more.

2 Cook the rice vermicelli in a large pot of boiling water until just done, about 3 to 5 minutes. Rinse in cold water and drain well. Set aside at room temperature for up to 2 hours.

3 Prepare a medium-hot fire in the grill.

4 Divide the lettuce, bean sprouts, basil, mint, and cilantro leaves, if using, among 4 large bowls. Separate the noodle strands and layer the noodles over the greens in the bowls.

5 Remove the shrimp from the marinade and thread the shrimp onto skewers or place in a grilling basket. Grill the shrimp about 3 inches from the fire for a minute or two on each side, just until they turn pink.

6 Arrange the shrimp over the noodles. Sprinkle with crushed peanuts and garnish with cilantro or basil sprigs. Serve at once with one or both of the dipping sauces.

NOTE: You can broil the shrimp if you don't wish to grill.

Smoked Shrimp
on Rice Vermicelli

YIELD: 4 MAIN-COURSE SERVINGS

The lightly smoked shrimp lend a surprisingly delicate flavor to this salad.

1 1/4 pounds large shrimp, in the shell, rinsed

12 ounces dried thin (1/8-inch) rice sticks or rice vermicelli

1/2 cup julienned scallion greens

1 red bell pepper, julienned

1/2 pound snow peas, julienned

1/2 cup Thai or sweet basil leaves

Lime Dressing

1/3 cup fresh lime juice

3 tablespoons Asian fish sauce

1 tablespoon minced fresh ginger

2 tablespoons palm sugar, or substitute light brown sugar

1 tablespoon peanut oil

1 Soak apple or hickory wood chips in water for at least 30 minutes. Prepare a medium-hot fire in a charcoal grill, with the rack set about 6 inches above the coals. When the coals are ash gray, place a layer of soaked chips over them. Lay the shrimp on the grill rack and cover the grill. Cook, turning once, until the shrimp are pink and firm, about 12 minutes. Remove from the grill. Peel and devein the shrimp.

2 Cook the rice noodles in a large pot of boiling water until just done, 3 to 5 minutes. Drain, rinse with cold water, and drain again.

3 To prepare the dressing, combine all the ingredients in a small saucepan. Heat, stirring, just until the sugar dissolves. Set aside to cool.

4 Combine the noodles, scallions, red pepper, snow peas, and basil in a serving dish. Pour the dressing over the salad. Toss gently. Lay the smoked shrimp around the salad and serve.

NOTE: If you are using a gas grill, place the wood chips in the chip holder and grill as above. If your grill doesn't have a chip holder, you can wrap the chips in heavy-duty aluminum foil, poke the package to create holes through which smoke can escape, and place the chips directly over the heating element. The shrimp may be placed directly on the grill, but to guarantee that none slip into the fire, you may want to lay the shrimp on a fish or vegetable grill rack that can be placed directly on the grill grate.

Jicama Shrimp Salad on **Glass Noodles**

YIELD: 4 MAIN-COURSE SERVINGS

The fresh cilantro, mint, and lime juice really perk up this dish.

8 ounces sweet potato starch glass vermicelli or 4 (1.75-ounce) skeins cellophane noodles

2 teaspoons toasted sesame oil

1 tablespoon soy sauce

3/4 pound medium shrimp

1/4 cup fresh lime juice

3 tablespoons Asian fish sauce

1 tablespoon sugar

2 teaspoons peanut or canola oil

2 tablespoons minced fresh cilantro

1 tablespoon minced fresh mint

2 cups julienned (1/4-inch) jicama

Garnish: Cilantro sprigs and lime wedges

1 *If using sweet potato starch vermicelli,* cover with boiling water and let stand for 10 minutes to soften. *If using cellophane noodles,* cover with hot tap water and let stand for 15 minutes to soften. Drain the noodles and rinse with cold water. Drain again. Scissor the noodles into 4-inch lengths.

2 In a small bowl, combine the sesame oil and soy sauce and pour over the noodles. Toss and refrigerate.

3 Bring a medium-size pot of water to boiling. Turn off the heat and add the shrimp. Let the shrimp poach for 3 minutes. Drain, plunge into cold water, drain again, and peel. Slice the shrimp in half lengthwise.

4 In a large bowl, combine the lime juice, fish sauce, and sugar. Stir to dissolve the sugar. Add the peanut oil, cilantro, mint, and jicama. Toss and add the shrimp. Refrigerate, covered, for an hour or more.

5 To serve, place a layer of noodles on individual salad plates. Top
   with the shrimp mixture. Garnish each with cilantro sprigs and
   lime wedges. Serve cold.

NOTE: I prefer the sweet potato starch noodles for this dish—
they do a better job of absorbing the flavors of the dressing.

Sichuan Noodle Salad
YIELD: 4 MAIN-COURSE SERVINGS

The combinations here are wonderfully balanced: the heat of the chiles with the coolness of the cucumber, and the Chinese roast pork with the sweet shrimp.

1/2 teaspoon minced ginger

2 teaspoons rice, Chinese black, or balsamic vinegar

1 tablespoon vegetable oil

1/2 pound cooked shrimp (about 1 1/2 cups)

1 recipe Sichuan Noodles (page 90)

1 cup julienned Chinese Roast Pork (page 204)

1 carrot, julienned

1 cucumber, julienned

2 fresh red serrano chile peppers, julienned

Leaf lettuce or Boston lettuce

1 In a small bowl, combine the ginger, vinegar, and vegetable oil. Add the cooked shrimp and marinate, covered, in the refrigerator for 30 minutes or longer.

2 Prepare the Sichuan Noodles according to the recipe directions.

3 In a large bowl, combine the Sichuan Noodles with the roast pork, carrot, cucumber, and chile peppers. Add the marinated shrimp and toss lightly. Chill well.

4 To serve, line a serving dish with lettuce leaves and fill the center with the noodle salad.

NOTE: If you live near a Chinese deli, you can substitute 6 ounces of commercial Chinese roast pork for your own homemade pork. Or, in a pinch, use a high-quality smoked turkey or ham.

Green Soba Salad

A salad of greens and green noodles makes a very refreshing dinner in hot weather. Pea shoots—the greens of the pea plant before it has produced pods—were once found only in Asian produce stores, but they have become commonplace in many specialty stores. The shoots are crisp, mild in flavor, and slightly sweet. They are worth seeking out, though another green such as spinach could be substituted. I like to make this salad with green tea soba noodles to add flavor and color.

1 pound dried soba noodles (plain or green tea)

2 tablespoons light miso

1/4 cup water

1/4 cup soy sauce

2 tablespoons rice vinegar

1 1/2 tablespoons toasted sesame oil

1 tablespoon minced fresh ginger

1/4 cup fresh lemon or lime juice

3 to 6 ounces snow pea shoots

3/4 cup diagonally sliced scallions, including green parts

1 Cook the soba noodles in 3 1/2 quarts of boiling water until just tender, about 5 to 7 minutes. Drain and rinse thoroughly to cool. Or use the *sashimizu* method: Bring a large pot of water to a boil. Add the noodles and cook for 2 minutes. Add 1 cup cold water and return to a boil. Repeat the process twice. Simmer the noodles until tender, about 5 minutes. Drain and rinse in cold water, rubbing the noodles together to remove the surface starch.

2 In a serving bowl, combine the miso, water, soy sauce, rice vinegar, sesame oil, ginger, and lemon or lime juice. Add the noodles, snow pea shoots, and scallions and toss lightly to mix. Serve cold or at room temperature.

Crabmeat Noodle Salad
with Asian Pesto Sauce

YIELD: 4 MAIN-COURSE SERVINGS

Fresh, unfrozen crabmeat makes all the difference in this very simple salad.

8 ounces dried rice vermicelli

8 ounces fresh crabmeat

1 cup Asian Pesto Sauce (page 214), at room temperature

2 cups shredded leaf lettuce or romaine

1 1/2 cups fresh mung bean sprouts (optional)

Garnish: Lime wedges

1 Cook the rice vermicelli in a large pot of boiling water until just done, about 3 to 5 minutes. Rinse in cold water and set aside in a sieve or colander to drain.

2 Pick through the crabmeat and discard any cartilage, keeping the crabmeat in chunks, as much as possible.

3 Combine the noodles and Asian pesto sauce. Gently fold in the crabmeat.

4 The salad may be served in individual bowls or one large serving dish. Layer the shredded lettuce and bean sprouts, if using, on the bottom, with the crabmeat noodle mixture on top. Serve cold, garnished with lime wedges.

Thai-Style Crab Salad
with Green Beans

YIELD: 4 MAIN-COURSE SERVINGS

This salad is especially nice made with the very thin Chinese long beans, if you can find them. Or substitute thin, young green beans.

3 (1.75-ounce) skeins cellophane noodles

1 pound thin green beans, cut into 1-inch pieces

1 pound fresh crabmeat, picked over

1 carrot, grated

1/4 cup fresh cilantro leaves

1/4 cup fresh mint leaves

1/4 cup finely sliced red onion

1 or 2 fresh hot red or green chiles, finely sliced

2 teaspoons minced fresh ginger

2 teaspoons minced garlic

1/4 cup fresh lime juice

3 tablespoons Asian fish sauce

2 tablespoons palm sugar, or substitute brown sugar

1 Cover the cellophane noodles with hot tap water and set aside to soften for 15 minutes. Drain in a colander, rinse with cold water, and drain well.

2 Steam the green beans over boiling water until just tender, 5 to 6 minutes. Drain. Plunge into cold water for a minute, then drain well.

3 Combine the crabmeat, carrot, cilantro, mint, onion, chiles, ginger, and garlic in a medium-size bowl. In a small bowl, combine the lime juice, fish sauce, and sugar, stirring to dissolve the sugar. Add to the salad ingredients and mix gently.

4 Make a bed on noodles on each individual serving plate. Top with the green beans and the crabmeat salad. Serve immediately.

NOTE: If you wish, you can prepare the noodles, crab salad, and beans ahead of time and keep in separate containers in the refrigerator. Assemble the salad just before serving.

Shredded Chicken Salad on **Glass Noodles**

YIELD: 4 MAIN-COURSE SERVINGS

Note the chiles in this dish, balanced by the fresh mint. I love the shredded Napa cabbage; it is so much more interesting in flavor and texture than lettuce.

4 boneless, skinless chicken breast halves

8 ounces sweet potato starch glass vermicelli or 4 (1.75-ounce) skeins cellophane noodles

2 teaspoons toasted sesame oil

1 tablespoon soy sauce

3 tablespoons fresh lime juice

3 tablespoons Asian fish sauce

1 tablespoon rice vinegar

1 tablespoon sugar

1 teaspoon minced garlic

2 tablespoons peanut or canola oil

1/2 teaspoon freshly ground black or white pepper

1/4 cup chopped fresh mint

2 fresh red serrano chiles, seeded and julienned, or Thai bird pepper, seeded and minced

2 scallions, including green parts, shredded in 2-inch strips

3 cups shredded Napa or Chinese cabbage (about 1/4 pound)

Freshly ground black pepper

Garnish: Mint or cilantro sprigs

1   Bring a medium-size pot of salted water to a boil. Add the chicken breasts, return the water to a boil, then reduce the heat to keep the water at a simmer. Cook for 15 minutes. Turn off the heat, cover the pot, and let the chicken stay in the water for 30 minutes. Remove the chicken from the pot and set aside. Reserve the broth for another use.

60

2   *If using sweet potato starch vermicelli,* cover the noodles with boiling water and set aside to soften for 10 minutes. *If using cellophane noodles,* cover the noodles with hot tap water and set aside to soften for 15 minutes. Drain the noodles, rinse with cold water, and drain again. Scissor the noodles into 4-inch lengths.

3   In a small bowl, combine the sesame oil and soy sauce and pour over the noodles. Toss and refrigerate.

4   When the chicken has partially cooled, place it in a bowl and use your fingers to finely shred it. You should have 3 cups shredded cooked chicken.

5   In a large bowl, combine the lime juice, fish sauce, rice vinegar, sugar, and garlic. Stir to dissolve the sugar. Add the peanut oil, pepper, and mint. Whisk together. Add the chicken, chiles, scallions, and cabbage. Add black pepper to taste. Toss to combine. Refrigerate, covered, until serving.

6   To serve, place a layer of noodles on individual salad plates or bowls, and divide the shredded chicken salad among them. Garnish each with mint or cilantro sprigs. Serve at once.

NOTE: Again, I prefer the sweet potato starch noodles for this dish—they do a better job of absorbing the flavors of the dressing.

Chicken Noodle Salad
with Peanuts
YIELD: 4 MAIN-COURSE SERVINGS

This rich spicy noodle dish is enhanced if you use a freshly ground natural peanut butter. You may vary the daikon used here with carrot or cucumber; or the scallions with chopped red onion.

1 (1-inch) piece fresh ginger, sliced

2 garlic cloves

6 tablespoons Chinese rice wine

1 pound boneless, skinless chicken breast

12 ounces dried wide flat Chinese egg noodles or fettuccine or linguine

2 tablespoons toasted sesame oil

3 tablespoons crunchy peanut butter

2 tablespoons soy sauce

1 1/2 tablespoons balsamic vinegar or rice wine vinegar

1 to 2 teaspoons chili paste with garlic or more to taste

2 tablespoons sugar or more to taste

1/4 pound snow peas, cut 1/4-inch thick on the diagonal

1 cup julienned daikon radish

1 cup sliced scallions, including green parts

1/2 cup chopped roasted unsalted peanuts

1 Bring a medium-size pot of salted water to a boil. Add the ginger, garlic, 4 tablespoons of the rice wine, and the chicken. Bring just to a boil, reduce the heat to low, and poach the chicken for 15 minutes. Cool in the cooking liquid.

2 Meanwhile, cook the noodles in plenty of boiling water until just done, about 5 minutes for Chinese egg noodles or vermicelli, 6 or 7 minutes for fettuccine. Drain and rinse under cold water. Toss with 1 tablespoon of the sesame oil.

3 With a whisk or in a blender, combine the peanut butter with 1/2 cup of the chicken cooking liquid. Add the remaining 2 tablespoons

rice wine, the remaining 1 tablespoon sesame oil, the soy sauce, vinegar, 1 teaspoon chili paste, and sugar. Blend well. Dip a noodle in the sauce to taste for seasoning, and add more chili paste and/or sugar as needed.

4 Remove the chicken from the cooking liquid and julienne.

5 In a large salad bowl, combine the chicken, noodles, and dressing. Toss well. Taste and adjust the seasonings, adding more soy sauce, vinegar, chili paste, or sugar as needed. Arrange the vegetables and peanuts over the top, sprinkle with the peanuts, and serve.

Tamarind-Glazed Pork
and Spicy Noodle Salad

YIELD: 4 TO 6 MAIN-COURSE SERVINGS

The sharp, sour sweetness of tamarind melds with the ginger and soy, giving the pork a flavorful glaze. Combined with the spicy ginger noodles, this is an intensely flavorful dish.

Pork and Marinade

2 tablespoons tamarind purée (pages 16-17)

1/4 cup hot water

1 teaspoon minced fresh ginger

2 teaspoons soy sauce

1 tablespoon peanut or canola oil

3/4 pound pork tenderloin, boneless pork loin, or 1-inch thick boneless pork chops

Salad

1/2 pound dried thin Chinese egg noodles or angel hair pasta (cappellini)

2 tablespoons toasted sesame oil

1 1/2 teaspoons chili paste with garlic, or more to taste

1 tablespoon minced fresh ginger

2 teaspoons minced garlic

2 tablespoons soy sauce

2 tablespoons rice vinegar

6 scallions, julienned

3/4 cup peeled julienned daikon radish

1 1/2 cups coarsely grated carrots (2 large carrots)

1 small red bell pepper, julienned

1 Prepare a medium-hot fire in a charcoal or gas grill with the rack set 3 to 4 inches above the coals.

2 To make the marinade, combine the tamarind and hot water in a small bowl. Stir and mash with a fork. Add the ginger, soy sauce,

and peanut oil. Stir well. Brush the marinade onto the pork. Refrigerate if holding for longer than 30 minutes.

3 Bring 2 quarts of water to boiling. Add the noodles and cook until just done, about 4 to 5 minutes. Drain and rinse with cold water. Scissor the noodles into 4-inch lengths. Toss with 1 tablespoon of the sesame oil and refrigerate.

4 Grill the pork to medium, or until an instant-read thermometer registers 150°–165°F, about 7 to 9 minutes per side for 1 piece of tenderloin or pork loin and 4 minutes per side for boneless chops. Let the pork stand for 10 minutes before slicing.

5 In a serving bowl, combine the remaining 1 tablespoon of sesame oil, chili paste, ginger, garlic, soy sauce, and rice vinegar. Add the scallions, daikon, carrots, red bell pepper, and the noodles. Toss to mix.

6 Slice the pork in thin slices and arrange over the spicy noodle salad. Serve at once.

NOTE: If you don't wish to grill the meat, you can roast it at 350°F. Allow about 40 minutes for tenderloin or loin; allow about 15 to 20 minutes for chops. Roast until a thermometer registers 160°F and allow the pork to stand for 10 minutes before slicing.

Thai Grilled Beef
and Rice Noodle Salad

YIELD: 6 MAIN-COURSE SERVINGS

Make the vegetables and noodles ahead, then grill the meat just before serving. This makes it an easy summer dish.

1 pound thin (1/8 inch) rice sticks or rice vermicelli

1/2 cup Asian fish sauce

1/3 cup lime juice (3 limes)

1/4 cup palm sugar, or substitute brown sugar

1 fresh red or green chile, chopped

1 carrot, peeled and shaved into curls

1 red bell pepper, julienned

1 cucumber, peeled, seeded, and thinly sliced

3/4 pound flank steak, sirloin, or other tender cut

1 tablespoon soy sauce

1 garlic clove, minced

1   Cook the rice noodles in a large pot of boiling water until just done, 3 to 5 minutes. Drain, rinse with cold water, and drain again. Place in a large serving bowl.

2   Combine the fish sauce, lime juice, sugar, and strips of chile in a small saucepan. Heat until the sugar dissolves. Set aside to cool.

3   Add the carrot, red bell pepper, and cucumber to the noodles. Pour the cooled fish sauce mixture over the salad. Toss well and set aside.

4   Prepare a medium-hot fire in a charcoal or gas grill, with the rack set 3 to 4 inches above the coals. Rub the beef with soy sauce and garlic. Grill the meat until it reaches the desired state of doneness. A 1/2-inch steak will take about 3 minutes per side for medium-rare. Let it rest for about 5 minutes, then slice into thin strips. If you don't wish to grill the beef, you can broil it either rare, medium, or well-done.

5   Divide the noodle salad among individual serving plates. Lay the strips of warm grilled steak over the noodles and serve at once.

Comforting Soups

Many Mushroom Soup
with Noodles and Greens
YIELD: 4 TO 6 MAIN-COURSE SERVINGS

The complex flavors of mushrooms have a chance to develop if the soup is made a few hours, or even a day, ahead, but add the greens just before serving. A hearty loaf of warm bread would complete this meal.

8 ounces fresh thin (1/4-inch) Chinese egg noodles

2 tablespoon peanut oil

1 tablespoon toasted sesame oil

1/4 cup chopped shallots

1 tablespoon minced garlic

3 scallions, including green parts, sliced 1-inch thick

3 tablespoons soy sauce

1/2 pound fresh button mushrooms, sliced 3/8-inch thick

1/4 pound fresh portobello mushrooms, caps sliced 3/8-inch thick and stems discarded

1/4 pound fresh shiitake mushrooms, caps sliced 3/8-inch thick and stems discarded

8 cups vegetable or chicken broth (pages 218–222)

Salt and freshly ground black pepper

4 cups bok choy, sliced 1 1/2 inches thick

1 To a large pot of salted boiling water, add the Chinese egg noodles, and over high heat return to a boil. Test the noodles at this point. They should be done. Drain and rinse in cold water. Drain again and set aside.

2 In a soup pot, combine the oils over medium heat and heat until hot but not smoking. Add the shallots, garlic, and scallions and sauté for 2 minutes. Add the soy sauce and mushrooms and sauté over very low heat, stirring at intervals, until the mushrooms have softened and some of their moisture has evaporated, about 10 minutes.

68

3 Add the broth and salt and black pepper and bring to a simmer for 20 minutes. Add the bok choy and simmer for 3 or 4 minutes, just until tender.

4 Divide the noodles among 4 to 6 large bowls. Ladle the hot soup over the noodles and serve.

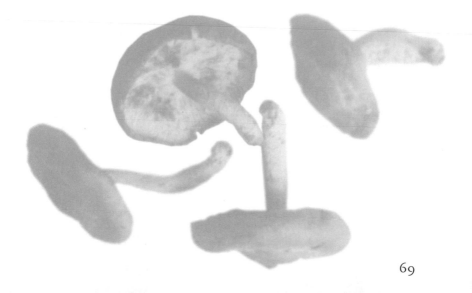

Ginger Garlic Noodle Bowl
with Shiitakes

YIELD: 4 MAIN-COURSE OR 6 FIRST-COURSE SERVINGS

I enjoy making this spicy soup in a relaxed way, tasting and adding chopped vegetables as I go along. Just put the chicken broth on the heat and add each ingredient as it is prepared. The aroma is enjoyable, and the garlic and ginger in this simple dish have good health benefits.

8 ounces dried thin Chinese egg noodles or angel hair pasta (cappellini)

6 cups Asian Vegetable Broth (page 218) or Homemade Chicken Broth (page 220)

3 tablespoons thinly sliced garlic (about 8 large cloves)

2 tablespoons chopped fresh ginger

1/2 cup thinly sliced scallions, including green parts

2 tablespoons chopped flat-leaf parsley

1 cup thinly sliced fresh shiitake or portobello mushroom caps

1/2 fresh red chile, thinly sliced

1 cup diced vegetables (such as carrot, celery with leaves, daikon, bok choy, or spinach)

1   Cook the Chinese egg noodles or angel hair pasta in plenty of boiling water until just done, about 4 to 5 minutes. Drain and rinse under cold water. Drain again and set aside.

2   In a large saucepan, bring the broth to a simmer and add the garlic, ginger, scallions, parsley, mushrooms, chile, and diced vegetables, as each is prepared. Simmer until the carrots or firmest vegetables are tender.

3   Divide the noodles among individual bowls. Add the hot broth with vegetables to the bowls. Serve immediately.

Roasted Garlic Glass Noodle Soup

YIELD: 4 TO 6 MAIN-COURSE SERVINGS

Roasted garlic has a subtle richness and flavor when simmered in a broth with a delicate miso. The cellophane noodles complete the light touch.

2 large firm garlic bulbs

2 (1.75-ounce) skeins cellophane noodles

2 tablespoons peanut oil

1 small onion, thinly sliced

1 tablespoon minced ginger

8 cups Asian Vegetable Broth (page 218) or Homemade Chicken Broth (page 220)

1/3 cup yellow or shiro (white) miso

Salt and freshly ground black pepper

Garnish: Finely sliced scallion

1 Preheat the oven to 375°F. Cut the top 1/4 inch off each garlic bulb, exposing the cloves. Place the garlic on a baking sheet. Roast until tender, about 40 minutes. Cool slightly, and squeeze each clove, extruding the roasted garlic pulp into a small dish.

2 Cover the cellophane noodles with hot tap water and set aside to soften for 15 minutes. Drain.

3 In a large heavy soup pot, heat the oil over medium heat and add the onion, ginger, and roasted garlic. Stir and cover the pot. "Sweat" the onion over a very low heat for about 10 minutes, until it becomes translucent.

4 Add the broth and miso; increase the heat and bring to a simmer. Maintain a simmer for 10 to 15 minutes.

5 Scissor the drained cellophane noodles into 2-inch pieces and add them to the soup. Season to taste with salt and black pepper. Serve hot, garnished with scallion slivers.

Miso Hotpot with Mushrooms and Udon

YIELD: 4 MAIN-COURSE SERVINGS

A traditional Japanese hotpot with miso broth and plump white udon noodles, mushrooms, tofu, and fresh vegetables is a filling one-bowl meal for a cold day. Look for the fat round udon noodles for this dish, but if they are not available, the flat udon noodles will be just fine.

6 ounces fresh or dried udon noodles

6 cups Dashi (page 215, or made from dashi concentrate)

1/4 cup shiro (white) miso

6 scallions, white parts, julienned; green parts, sliced thin diagonally

1 small carrot, shaved lengthwise with a vegetable peeler into long strips

4 ounces fresh or canned nameko mushrooms, rinsed, or 3 ounces fresh shiitakes, stems removed and caps sliced and 1 1/2 ounces enoki mushrooms, ends trimmed

2 cups small spinach leaves

6 ounces firm tofu, sliced into thin pieces

Shichimi (Japanese seven-spice powder)

1   *If you are using dried udon noodles,* bring a medium-size pot of water to a boil. Add the noodles and stir to separate. When the water returns to a boil, cook the udon at a brisk boil for about 10 minutes, stirring intermittently, until the noodles are a little softer than al dente. Drain and rinse under cold water. Return the noodles to the pan and soak them in cool water to cover for 10 to 15 minutes, to allow them to expand and soften further. Drain and set aside.

If you are using cooked packaged udon noodles, simply add them to boiling water for a minute to heat them through, then drain. Discard the flavoring packets, which usually contain MSG.

2   In a large saucepan, bring the broth to a simmer. Add the miso, scallions, carrot, and mushrooms. Simmer for 2 or 3 minutes, just below the boiling point, until the scallions are tender. Add the spinach and tofu, and simmer for a minute or two until hot.

3 To serve, divide the noodles among individual bowls and ladle the broth and vegetables over the noodles. Serve hot, with *shichimi* as a table condiment.

NOTE: *Shichimi*, or Japanese seven-spice powder, is a mixture of several spices and flavors. It includes sansho, which is ground Sichuan peppercorns, ground chiles, hemp seeds, dried orange peel, flakes of nori, white sesame seeds, and white poppy seeds. It is available in small jars in Asian markets.

Dashi with Udon Noodles and Vegetables

YIELD: 4 MAIN-COURSE SERVINGS

In this satisfying soup, plump udon noodles are combined with vegetables and seaweed in a dashi broth.

3-inch-square piece dried kombu seaweed, wiped with a damp cloth

6 medium-size dried shiitake mushroom caps

8 ounces udon noodles

4 cups Dashi (page 215, or made from dashi concentrate)

1/2 cup sliced scallions

1/4 pound spinach leaves (about 4 cups)

3 cups sliced Napa cabbage (about 5 ounces)

1 Soak the kombu in warm water to cover for 15 minutes. Drain and slice into 1/4-inch pieces. Slice these in half and set aside.

2 Soak the dried shiitakes in hot water to cover for 20 to 30 minutes. Drain and squeeze the mushrooms dry. Quarter the mushroom caps and set aside.

3 *If you are using dried udon noodles,* bring a medium-size pot of water to a boil. Add the noodles and stir to separate. When the water returns to a boil, cook the udon at a brisk boil for about 10 minutes, stirring intermittently, until the noodles are a little softer than al dente. Drain, and rinse under cold water. Return the noodles to the pan and soak them in cool water to cover for 10 to 15 minutes, to allow them to expand and soften further. Drain and set aside.

If you are using cooked packaged udon noodles, simply add them to boiling water for a minute to heat them through, then drain. Discard the flavoring packets, which usually contain MSG.

4 In a large saucepan, bring the dashi broth to a simmer. Add the scallions, spinach, cabbage, and shiitakes. Simmer for 2 or 3 minutes, just below the boiling point, until the cabbage is tender. Add the kombu slices and turn off the heat. Divide the noodles

among the individual bowls and ladle the broth and vegetables over the noodles. Serve right away.

Long-Life Noodle Soup

Traditionally, this soup is part of a Chinese birthday celebration meal. Guests slurp up the soup without breaking the noodles, long noodles meaning a long life for the honoree. A rich homemade chicken broth is essential here.

6 dried shiitake mushrooms

6 ounces fresh Chinese egg noodles

1/2 pound scallops

1/2 pound shrimp, shelled and deveined

1/4 pound Chinese Roast Pork (page 204) or ham

1/4 pound snow peas

1 teaspoon toasted sesame oil

1 teaspoon peanut oil

1 teaspoon minced fresh ginger

2 scallions, thinly sliced on the diagonal

6 cups Homemade Chicken Broth (page 220)

3 tablespoons mushroom soy sauce or soy sauce

1/2 teaspoon salt

Freshly ground black pepper

1   In a small bowl, soak the shiitakes in hot water to cover for 20 to 30 minutes. Squeeze the mushrooms dry, discard the stems, and slice the caps thinly.

2   To a large pot of salted boiling water, add the Chinese egg noodles, and over high heat return to a boil. Test the noodles at this point. They should be done. Drain and rinse in cold water. Drain well and set aside.

3   Halve the scallops. Bring 1 1/2 quarts of water to a boil. Add the scallops and shrimp, and cook for 1 minute, just until they turn color but are not completely cooked through. Drain the scallops and shrimp and set aside.

4 Cut the pork into matchstick strips. String the snow peas and halve diagonally.

5 Place a large soup pot over high heat for 30 seconds. Add the sesame and peanut oils, swirl to coat the pan, and heat until hot but not smoking. Add the ginger and scallions and stir-fry for 1 minute. Add the mushrooms and snow peas; stir-fry for 1 minute. Add the chicken broth and bring to a boil. Add the noodles, shrimp, scallops, and half the pork. Stir in the soy sauce, salt, and black pepper and taste for seasoning.

6 Serve the soup, hot, in a large serving bowl or covered dish, with the remaining pork sprinkled on top.

Sweet and Sour Shrimp Noodle Soup

YIELD: 4 MAIN-COURSE SERVINGS

A vibrantly flavored soup—not for the timid.

8 ounces dried rice vermicelli

1 teaspoon toasted sesame oil

3 large stalks lemongrass

1 tablespoon peanut oil

1 Thai red bird chile or red serrano chile, minced (or more)

3 scallions, cut in 1-inch pieces

4 cups Homemade Chicken Broth (page 220)

6 kaffir lime leaves, sliced

2 tablespoons Asian fish sauce

1/2 teaspoon sugar

1 teaspoon salt

1/2 pound large shrimp, peeled and deveined, tails left on

1 cup well-drained canned straw mushrooms, rinsed

Juice of 1 lime (about 2 1/2 tablespoons)

1/2 teaspoon freshly ground black pepper

Garnish: Cilantro leaves

1 To a large pot of boiling salted water, add the rice vermicelli, and over high heat return to a boil. Cook for 3 to 5 minutes, until just done. Drain and rinse with cold water. Drain and toss with sesame oil. Set aside.

2 Trim the lemongrass stalks of the outer leaves. Cut away the tops, leaving the inner lower portion, about 6 inches long. Cut away the hard root section below the inner stalk. With a heavy knife or cleaver, crush the stalks at intervals on all sides and cut them into 2-inch chunks.

3 Heat a large skillet over high heat for 30 seconds. Add the peanut oil, swirl to coat the pan, and heat until hot but not smoking. Add the chiles, scallions, and lemongrass and stir-fry for 2 minutes.

78

Add the broth, kaffir lime leaves, fish sauce, sugar, and salt and bring to a simmer. Simmer for 15 minutes. Remove the lemongrass.

4 Add the shrimp, mushrooms, lime juice, and black pepper. Simmer for 1 minute. Add the rice noodles. Serve hot, with cilantro leaves scattered over the soup.

NOTE: Kaffir lime leaves can be found in Asian markets. Stock up on the leaves and store them in your freezer in a zippered plastic bag. Dried leaves do not have the fragrance and flavor needed in this soup.

Shrimp-Spinach Wontons in **Lemony Broth**

This is not your typical American-Chinese restaurant wonton soup, despite a few superficial similarities. The Lemony Chicken Broth adds a fresh twist to this old favorite.

1 quarter-size slice ginger

1 garlic clove

2 scallions, including some green parts

1/2 pound raw shrimp, shelled and deveined

1/4 pound ground pork

1 tablespoon oyster sauce

1 tablespoon rice wine or sherry

1 1/2 teaspoons mirin or 3/4 teaspoon sugar

2 teaspoons soy sauce

2 teaspoons toasted sesame oil

2 cups chopped spinach

About 32 wonton wrappers

1 egg, beaten

Lemony Chicken Broth (page 221)

1/4 pound Chinese broccoli (*gai-lon*) or Napa cabbage, sliced 1-inch thick

Garnishes: Chopped scallions, toasted sesame oil, soy sauce, and Hot Chili Oil (page 223)

1   Mince the ginger and garlic in a food processor. Add the scallions and mince. Turn into a medium-size bowl. Dry the shrimp on paper toweling, add to the processor, and mince briefly. Add the shrimp and ground pork to the bowl and combine with the oyster sauce, rice wine, mirin, and soy sauce.

2   In a small skillet, heat the sesame oil over medium heat until hot. Add the spinach and stir-fry until wilted, about 1 minute. Take off the heat. Cool for a minute and combine with the shrimp and pork mixture.

3 To fill the wrappers, place 1 heaping teaspoon of filling off center
   on each wrapper. Brush the edge of half the wrapper with beaten
   egg and bring two points together, sealing tightly. Then bring the
   two side points together and press them tightly, forming a cap
   shape. Keep the wontons covered with plastic wrap to prevent drying out.

4 Bring a large pot of salted water to a boil and add 10 or 12 wontons.
   Keep the water simmering, but not boiling, and cook the wontons
   for about 5 minutes, until just tender. Remove carefully with a flat
   Chinese strainer and drain them. They may be refrigerated at this
   point for a few hours, covered with plastic wrap.

5 In a medium-size saucepan, heat the broth with the greens.

6 To serve, place 5 or 6 wontons in each bowl and pour some of the
   hot broth with greens over them. Serve with chopped scallions,
   toasted sesame oil, soy sauce, and hot chili oil on the table, so that
   people may help themselves.

Chicken and Coconut Soup with Lemongrass

YIELD: 4 MAIN-COURSE OR 6 FIRST-COURSE SERVINGS

Generously seasoned with lemongrass, cilantro, and fish sauce, the flavors of Thai cooking are beautifully balanced in this coconut milk-based soup. If you like your food spicy, the incendiary bird's-eye chiles are the hot peppers of choice. But if you don't care for spicy hot foods, omit the hot peppers and you will still enjoy this wonderful soup.

4 ounces thin (1/8-inch) rice sticks or rice vermicelli

2 stalks fresh lemongrass (bottom 6 inches only), trimmed and thinly sliced, or 1/4 cup chopped frozen lemongrass

3 tablespoons fresh ginger

3 large garlic cloves

2 tablespoons chopped fresh cilantro roots

8 shallots

1 3/4 cups fresh coconut milk or 1 (14-ounce) can

1/2 pound boneless skinless chicken breast, cut in 1/2-inch strips

3 cups chicken broth (pages 220-222)

Juice of 1 lime

2 tablespoons Asian fish sauce

Freshly ground white or black pepper

1 to 2 fresh red chiles, seeded and minced (optional)

Garnish: Cilantro sprigs and finely shredded kaffir lime leaves

1 Cover the rice noodles with boiling water and set aside to soak for 15 minutes. Drain and rinse under cold water. Drain again and set aside.

2 With the food processor running, combine the lemongrass, ginger, garlic, cilantro roots, and shallots. Process until finely chopped.

3 In a medium-size saucepan, bring the coconut milk to a simmer over medium heat. Add the lemongrass mixture and stir well. Add

the chicken and broth. Return the soup to a simmer. Reduce the heat and simmer until the chicken is tender, 5 to 8 minutes.

4 Add the softened rice vermicelli, lime juice, fish sauce, and pepper to taste. Add the minced chilies, if you want the soup spicy. Taste and adjust the seasonings.

5 Serve hot, in individual bowls, garnished with cilantro and kaffir lime leaves.

Pho Bo (Vietnamese Beef and Noodle Soup)

Pho is Vietnam's beloved comfort food. There are street stalls and diners that sell only pho—in Vietnam and wherever one finds a community of expatriated Vietnamese. Pho may be eaten anytime of the day, especially for breakfast. Like the Western chicken noodle soup, this soup has as many variations as cooks—but it is always served with a plate of fresh herbs and greens, which are added to taste and just barely cooked in the steaming hot broth.

1 pound dried flat (1/4-inch) rice sticks

1/2 pound beef sirloin

1/4 cup Asian fish sauce

Freshly ground black pepper

3 scallions, sliced thin

1 onion, sliced very thin

1/3 cup fresh cilantro, chopped

Stock

4 to 5 pounds beef chuck

6 quarts water

2 large onions, peeled

2 (3-inch) pieces fresh ginger, unpeeled

8 star anise

6 whole cloves

2 tablespoons salt

2 parsnips, cut in 1-inch chunks

Accompaniments

2 cups fresh mung bean sprouts

1 cup fresh Thai or sweet basil leaves

1 cup fresh mint leaves

2 Thai or serrano chile peppers, sliced thinly

2 limes, cut into wedges

1 Trim the beef chuck of all fat and cut into 4 or 5 pieces. Bring a large stockpot of water to a boil and add the beef. Bring to a boil and simmer for 5 minutes. Drain the water out and rinse the stockpot. Add the beef and 6 quarts of water to the stockpot and return to a boil. Reduce the heat to a simmer and skim the surface of any residue.

2 While the stock is simmering, heat a medium skillet for a minute and char the onions and ginger in the dry pan, turning a few times. This will take about 5 minutes.

3 Add the onions, ginger, anise, cloves, salt, and parsnips to the broth and continue simmering for about 2 hours. Remove the onions, anise, cloves, and parsnips and continue simmering the beef and ginger for another hour or more, until the broth has absorbed full flavor.

4 While the broth is simmering, cover the rice stick noodles with warm tap water and set aside to soften for 30 minutes. Drain and set aside.

5 Meanwhile, prepare the accompaniments and arrange on a large plate. Slice the sirloin into very thin pieces across the grain.

6 Before serving, bring a large pot of water to a boil. Drain the noodles and add to the boiling water. Cook until just done, about 2 to 3 minutes.

7 Remove the beef chuck from the broth and freeze for another use. Add the fish sauce to the broth and continue simmering.

8 Heat the soup bowls. Drain the noodles and divide the noodles among the bowls. Top each with sliced sirloin, black pepper, scallions, onion slices, and cilantro. Ladle the hot broth over the beef and raw vegetables (the hot broth will cook them). Serve the accompaniments with the soup, so that each diner may top the soup with fresh greens and lime juice.

NOTE: To make a good pho, it is necessary to make a quantity of broth. Freeze some for later use. In Vietnam, oxtails would be used to make the broth, but chuck is more readily available in the U.S. For ease in slicing, freeze the sirloin for 30 minutes first.

Vegetarians'
Delight

Baked Noodle Pancake
YIELD: 4 TO 6 SIDE-DISH SERVINGS

As an alternative to rice with a stir-fry, this foolproof noodle cake is easy to make.

3/4 pound fresh Chinese wheat flour noodles

1 tablespoon toasted sesame oil

3 tablespoons peanut oil

1 Preheat the oven to 500°F.

2 Cook the Chinese wheat flour noodles in plenty of boiling water until just done, about 5 to 7 minutes. Drain, rinse with cold water, and drain again.

3 Turn the noodles into a large bowl. Add the sesame oil and 1 tablespoon of the peanut oil. Toss the noodles to distribute the oil.

4 Place a large (12-inch) pizza pan in the oven for 5 minutes. Remove the pan and pour in 2 tablespoons of peanut oil, swirling the pan to coat it completely with the oil.

5 Spread the noodles over the pan and pat to form an even cake. Place the pan on the bottom rack of the oven and bake, uncovered, until lightly browned, about 20 minutes or more.

6 Cut into 4 or 6 pieces and serve hot with a stir-fried dish.

Hot Chili Noodles

YIELD: 4 MAIN-COURSE OR 6 TO 8 SIDE-DISH SERVINGS

For those who take their noodles hot, this is a spicy one! The sweet-hot flavors of my homemade Chili Dipping Sauce are particularly pleasing in this combination, but you can substitute any Asian chili sauce.

12 ounces dried thin Chinese egg noodles

2 teaspoons toasted sesame oil

2-inch piece ginger, chopped

1 large garlic clove

3 medium shallots

4 red or green serrano or jalapeño chiles, including the seeds

1/4 cup Chili Dipping Sauce (page 211) or Asian chili sauce

1 tablespoon peanut or canola oil

1 cup finely shredded scallions, including green parts (optional)

1/2 cup grated carrot (optional)

1/4 cup water

1 Cook the Chinese egg noodles in a large pot of boiling water for 4 to 5 minutes, until just done. Drain and toss with 1 teaspoon of the sesame oil.

2 Combine the ginger, garlic, shallots, chiles, and chili sauce in a food processor and grind to a chunky pesto-like consistency.

3 Place a wok or large skillet over high heat for 30 seconds. Add the remaining 1 teaspoon sesame oil and the peanut oil, swirl to coat the pan, and heat until hot but not smoking. Add the chili paste and stir-fry for 2 minutes until fragrant.

4 Add the noodles, scallions, carrot, if using, and water and stir-fry for about 2 or 3 minutes. Serve hot.

Sichuan Noodles

Sichuan peppercorns are the aromatic red-brown seeds that give this dish its particular flavor. These seeds are from a prickly ash tree known as fagara, *and are not at all related to the familiar black pepper found on Western tables. Not only is the flavor more lemony and aromatic, it lacks the heat of a Western peppercorn. If you can't find Sichuan peppercorns, look for Japanese* sansho *which is made from the same seeds, ground to a powder.*

1 tablespoon Sichuan peppercorns

1 tablespoon minced garlic

2 teaspoons minced ginger

1/4 cup dark soy sauce

2 tablespoons toasted sesame oil

1 to 2 tablespoons Hot Chili Oil (for homemade, see page 223)

3 tablespoons Chinese black vinegar or balsamic vinegar

1 tablespoon sugar

12 ounces fresh Chinese wheat flour noodles, Chinese flat egg noodles, or fettuccine

1/4 cup chopped scallions

1   Toast the Sichuan peppercorns in a dry skillet for 1 to 2 minutes over medium heat, until aromatic, shaking the pan and watching it carefully to avoid scorching. Cool slightly, then grind the peppercorns in a pepper or spice mill, or with a mortar and pestle.

2   To make the sauce, combine the garlic, ginger, soy sauce, sesame oil, chili oil, vinegar, and sugar in a large bowl. Stir to dissolve the sugar. Add the ground peppercorns. Cover and set aside.

3   Bring a large pot of water to a boil over high heat. Add the noodles and cook until just done, about 5 to 7 minutes. Drain and rinse under cold water. Allow to drain in a sieve or colander for 2 or 3 minutes.

4 Combine the noodles and scallions with the sauce in the bowl, and toss well. Serve cold or at room temperature.

NOTE: You'll find Sichuan peppercorns come in fairly large quantities, but don't worry about storage. They will keep for several years without loss of flavor, as long as you store them in a cool, dark, dry place.

Hot and Sour Pepper Noodles
YIELD: 4 TO 6 MAIN-COURSE SERVINGS

This dish is triply hot—from fresh chiles, black pepper, and black bean sauce with chili—but it is the freshly ground black pepper that accounts for the defining flavor.

1 pound fresh Chinese wheat flour noodles

1 large fresh chile pepper or 2 jalapeño peppers, seeded and minced

1 tablespoon freshly ground black pepper

2 tablespoons black bean sauce with chili

3 tablespoons hoisin sauce

1 1/2 tablespoons toasted sesame oil

2 tablespoons Chinese black, balsamic, or rice vinegar

3 scallions, including green parts, sliced 1/4-inch thick (about 1/2 cup)

1 carrot, julienned (about 1 cup)

1/4 small red cabbage, julienned (about 1 1/2 cups)

1 Cook the Chinese wheat flour noodles in a large pot of boiling water until just done, about 5 to 7 minutes. Drain and rinse with hot water. Drain. You may wish to scissor the noodles into 5- or 6-inch lengths.

2 Combine the fresh chile, black pepper, black bean sauce, hoisin sauce, sesame oil, and vinegar in a small bowl or mini processor.

3 Stir the sauce into the hot noodles. Add the scallions, carrot, and cabbage to the noodles and mix well. Serve hot or at room temperature.

Coconut Curry Noodles
YIELD: 4 MAIN-COURSE OR 6 TO 8 SIDE-DISH SERVINGS

Coconut-milk curries are typical of Malaysian and Thai cooking.

2 teaspoons toasted sesame oil

1 tablespoon minced ginger

1/2 cup chopped red onion or scallions

2 teaspoons curry powder (Madras curry powder is recommended)

1/2 cup toasted unsalted cashew pieces (2 ounces)

1 cup coconut milk

3 tablespoons fresh lime juice

1/2 teaspoon salt

1/2 cup fresh cilantro leaves

10 ounces dried rice vermicelli or thin (1/8-inch) rice stick noodles

3 cups snow peas or small sugar snap peas (about 3/4 pound)

Garnish: Wedges of lime and cilantro sprigs

1 Place a large nonstick skillet or wok over medium heat for 30 seconds. Add the sesame oil, swirl to coat the pan, and heat until hot but not smoking. Add the ginger, onion, and curry powder. Sauté until the onion begins to soften, about 2 to 3 minutes. Add the cashews; sauté for 1 minute. Add the coconut milk, lime juice, and salt. Bring to a simmer and add the cilantro leaves. Set aside.

2 Cook the rice noodles and snow peas together in a large pot of boiling water until the noodles are just done, about 5 minutes. Drain.

3 Combine the noodles and snow peas with the coconut curry sauce and serve immediately garnished with lime wedges and cilantro sprigs.

VARIATION: Cooked chicken or shrimp could be added with the coconut milk.

Hot Green Noodles

These noodles are really hot with the fresh flavors of cilantro and lemongrass. They make a delicious side dish alongside seafood and are even better the next day reheated in the microwave.

8 ounces dried thin (1/8-inch) rice stick noodles

1 teaspoon toasted sesame oil

2 stalks lemongrass, trimmed and lower 6 inches minced, or 1/4 cup chopped frozen lemongrass

1 large garlic clove, roughly chopped

2 green jalapeño peppers, including the seeds of 1 pepper, chopped

4 scallions, including green parts, roughly chopped

2 cups cilantro (leaves, stems, and any root included)

1/2 teaspoon salt

1 teaspoon freshly ground white or black pepper

3/4 cup coconut milk

1 tablespoon peanut or canola oil

3 tablespoons fresh lime juice

Garnish: Cilantro sprigs

1   Break the rice noodles in half and soak in boiling water to cover for 15 minutes, until softened. Drain and toss with toasted sesame oil.

2   Combine the lemongrass, garlic, jalapeño peppers, scallions, cilantro, salt, pepper, and 1/4 cup of the coconut milk in a food processor. Grind to a chunky pesto-like consistency.

3   Heat a wok or large skillet over high heat for 30 seconds. Add the peanut oil, swirl to coat the pan, and heat until hot but not smoking. Add the lemongrass mixture and stir-fry for 2 or 3 minutes. Add the remaining 1/2 cup coconut milk and the lime juice. Continue cooking for a minute. Add the noodles and toss until heated through. Serve immediately, garnished with cilantro sprigs.

Ginger Noodles

These noodles have lots of ginger flavor. They make a lovely side dish with grilled fish or chicken.

3 (1.75-ounce) skeins cellophane noodles

1 1/2 tablespoons toasted sesame oil

1 cup halved and very thinly sliced red onion

3 tablespoons minced fresh ginger

2 tablespoons finely shredded pickled ginger

2 tablespoons mirin

1 tablespoon rice vinegar

1/2 teaspoon salt

2 tablespoons cut chives

1 1/2 cups fresh mung bean sprouts

1   Cover the cellophane noodles with hot tap water and set aside to soften for 15 minutes. Drain the noodles and rinse with cold water. Scissor into 3-inch lengths and set aside.

2   Place a wok or large skillet over high heat for 30 seconds. Add the sesame oil, swirl to coat the pan, and heat until hot but not smoking. Add the onion and fresh ginger and stir-fry until the onion has wilted, about 3 minutes. Remove from the heat.

3   Add the pickled ginger, mirin, rice vinegar, and salt. Stir well. Add the cellophane noodles, chives, and mung bean sprouts and toss until well mixed. Serve at room temperature or lightly warmed.

NOTE: Pickled ginger is found wherever Japanese foods are sold. The ginger root is thinly sliced, then preserved in brine, rice wine, or rice vinegar. The preserving process turns the ginger pink. Pickled ginger is often used as a garnish.

Spicy Hunan Noodles

YIELD: 4 MAIN-COURSE OR 6 TO 8 SIDE-DISH SERVINGS

This is a quick and easy dish to put together. It is served cold, so it is good for hot-weather dining, or when you are putting together a menu of several different dishes. The vegetables can be varied with sliced blanched snow peas, grated daikon, julienned chile pepper—whatever you have on hand.

1 pound fresh or dried Chinese wheat flour noodles

3 tablespoons toasted sesame oil

3 tablespoons hoisin sauce

2 tablespoons soy sauce

2 tablespoons rice vinegar

1 to 1 1/2 tablespoons hot chili oil (page 223)

1 teaspoon minced fresh ginger

1/2 cup chopped scallions

1 cup grated carrot (about 2 carrots)

1 small red bell pepper, grated

Salt and freshly ground black pepper

1 Break the dried Chinese wheat flour noodles into 4-inch lengths, or scissor fresh noodles into 4-inch lengths. Cook the noodles in a large pot of boiling water until just done, about 5 to 7 minutes. Drain and rinse under cold water. Drain again. Toss the noodles with the sesame oil and set aside.

2 In a small bowl, combine the hoisin sauce, soy sauce, rice vinegar, hot chili oil, and ginger. Pour the sauce over the noodles and toss to combine. Chill the noodles.

3 One or two hours before serving, add the scallions, carrots, and red bell pepper. Season to taste with salt and black pepper. Serve cold.

NOTE: A quality hoisin sauce is critical to the flavor of this dish. My favorite brand is Koon Chun.

Dashi Noodle Bowl
with Fresh Vegetables
YIELD: 4 MAIN-COURSE SERVINGS

The crunch and flavors of the barely cooked vegetables pair nicely with the chewy noodles.

1 broccoli spear (about 8 ounces)

8 ounces dried soba noodles

4 teaspoons toasted sesame oil

2 teaspoons minced fresh ginger

1 teaspoon chopped garlic

2/3 cup sliced scallions

1/4 cup sliced cilantro leaves

2 1/2 cups julienned Napa or Chinese cabbage

3 cups Shiitake Dashi (available where Japanese foods are sold)

Garnish: Cilantro sprigs

1   Peel the broccoli stem and cut into 1/4-inch dice. Cut the flowers into bite-size pieces. Bring a medium-size pot of water to a boil and add the broccoli stems. Boil for 2 minutes. Add the florets and boil for 1 minute. Drain and cover the broccoli with cold water. Drain again and set aside.

2   Cook the soba noodles in a large pot of salted boiling water over high heat until just done, about 5 to 7 minutes. Drain well. Or, to cook by the *sashimizu* method, bring a large pot of water to a boil. Add the noodles and cook for 2 minutes. Add 1 cup of cold water and return to a boil. Repeat the process twice. Simmer the noodles until tender, about 5 minutes. Drain well.

3   Divide the noodles among 4 large bowls. Add about 1 teaspoon sesame oil to each bowl of noodles. Divide the ginger, garlic, scallions, cilantro, shredded cabbage, and broccoli among the bowls.

4   Heat the shiitake dashi to boiling and pour over the vegetables and noodles. Garnish each bowl with cilantro sprigs and serve hot.

Chapchae

(KOREAN GLASS NOODLES WITH VEGETABLES)

YIELD: 4 MAIN-COURSE SERVINGS

The key to this dish is not to overcook the noodles. They should have a pleasing chewiness. Korean glass vermicelli, made from sweet potato starch, are fatter and more translucent than Chinese or Vietnamese cellophane noodles, which are made from mung beans, but either noodle will work just fine in this recipe.

1/2 ounce dried black fungus (cloud or wood ear mushrooms) (about 3/4 cup)

8 ounces sweet potato starch glass noodles or 4 (1.75-ounce) skeins cellophane noodles

3 tablespoons soy sauce

1 tablespoon peanut oil

2 teaspoons toasted sesame oil

1 teaspoon hot chili oil (page 223)

2 garlic cloves, minced

1 red onion, sliced vertically into slivers

2 carrots, julienned (about 1 1/4 cups)

1/2 pound small spinach leaves

2 teaspoons sesame seeds, toasted

1 Soak the dried black fungus in warm water for 25 minutes. Drain the fungus, bundle, and slice into a thin julienne.

2 *If using sweet potato starch noodles,* break the noodles into 4-inch lengths. Cover the noodles with boiling water and set aside to soften for 10 minutes. *If using cellophane noodles,* cover the noodles with hot tap water and set aside to soften for 15 minutes. Drain the noodles and rinse in cold water. Leave draining in a sieve or colander for 2 or 3 minutes. Turn into a bowl, and *if using cellophane noodles,* scissor them into 4-inch lengths. Add 1 tablespoon of the soy sauce to the noodles. Toss until mixed through, and set aside.

3 Place a wok or large skillet over high heat for 30 seconds. Add the peanut, sesame, and chili oils, swirl to coat the pan, and heat until

hot but not smoking. Add the garlic, onion, and carrots and stir-fry for 3 to 4 minutes, until the vegetables begin to soften. Add the remaining 2 tablespoons soy sauce and black fungus and stir-fry for 2 minutes.

4 Add the noodles and the spinach and stir-fry until the noodles are hot and have absorbed the flavors. Serve immediately, sprinkled with toasted sesame seeds.

VARIATION: Chapchae can also be made adding thin pieces of beef, stir-fried with the vegetables.

Savory Noodles with Orange Peel and Shiitakes

YIELD: 4 MAIN-COURSE OR 6 TO 8 SIDE-DISH SERVINGS

Orange zest, ginger, and chili paste tossed with shiitakes, tofu, and noodles make this an intensely flavorful dish, set off with crunchy toasted sesame seeds.

1/2 pound firm tofu

12 ounces dried thin Chinese egg noodles or angel hair pasta

2 teaspoons toasted sesame oil

6 tablespoons soy sauce

1/3 cup fresh orange juice

1/4 cup rice wine or dry sherry

1 tablespoon chili paste with garlic

1 tablespoon peanut oil

Zest of 1 thin-skinned juice orange, julienned

2 tablespoons minced fresh ginger

1 tablespoon minced garlic

6 ounces fresh shiitake mushroom caps, sliced (about 2 cups)

Approximately 12 scallions, julienned (about 1 1/2 cups)

1 fresh red chile, finely shredded (optional)

3 tablespoons sesame seeds

1 Cut the tofu into 1-inch-thick slices. Wrap in a dish towel and press with a weight to drain off excess water (see page 21). Cut into 1/2-inch cubes.

2 Cook the Chinese egg noodles in a large pot of boiling water until tender but still firm, about 4 to 5 minutes. Drain and mix with the sesame oil.

3 Combine the soy sauce, orange juice, rice wine, and chili paste in a small bowl and blend well. Set aside.

4 Place a wok or large skillet over high heat for about 30 seconds. Add the peanut oil, swirl to coat the pan, and heat until hot but not smoking. Add the orange peel. Stir-fry for 1 minute, then add the ginger, garlic, mushrooms, scallions, chile, if using, tofu, and orange juice mixture. Continue stir-frying until the mushrooms are tender, about 3 to 4 minutes. Add the noodles and toss gently until the noodles are hot. Place in a warm serving dish.

5 Wipe out the skillet or wok and return to the heat. Lightly toast the sesame seeds for about 2 minutes. Sprinkle over the noodles and serve hot.

Stir-Fried Vegetables and Bean Curd on Chinese Noodles

YIELD: 4 MAIN-COURSE SERVINGS

Have the ingredients measured out in small bowls before you begin stir-frying, and the dish will go together in short order. The noodles soak up the juices and the flavors, and they are also delicious rewarmed the next day—if you have any left!

10 ounces fresh Chinese wheat flour noodles or dried fettuccine or linguine

3 teaspoons toasted sesame oil

12 ounces firm tofu

3 tablespoons peanut oil

1 tablespoon minced garlic

6 scallions, cut in 1-inch pieces, or 2 leeks, white part only, shredded

2 stalks lemongrass, trimmed and bottom 6 inches minced, or 1/4 cup frozen chopped lemongrass

1/2 red bell pepper, cut in 3/4-inch cubes

1 carrot, thinly sliced

1 1/2 cups snow peas

3 ounces fresh shiitake mushrooms, stems removed, caps sliced (about 1 cup)

1 1/2 cups fresh bean sprouts

1 cup baby corn (optional)

2 medium-size firm tomatoes, each cut in 8 wedges (optional)

6 tablespoons hoisin sauce

3 tablespoons soy sauce

Freshly ground black pepper

Approximately 1/2 cup vegetable broth or chicken broth (pages 218–222)

1 Cook the Chinese wheat flour noodles in a large pot of boiling water until tender but still firm, about 5 to 7 minutes. (If using

fettuccine or linguine, cook according to the package directions.)
Drain and mix with 2 teaspoons of the sesame oil.

2   Cut the tofu blocks across diagonally. Then slice the triangles into
3/8-inch-thick slices.

3   Place a wok or large skillet over high heat for about 30 seconds.
Add 2 tablespoons of the peanut oil, swirl to coat the pan, and heat
until hot but not smoking. Add the tofu and stir-fry until lightly
brown and crisp, about 5 minutes. Scoop the tofu out of the wok
with a flat strainer and set aside.

4   Add the remaining 1 tablespoon peanut oil and 1 teaspoon sesame
oil to the oil remaining in the wok and heat over high heat until
hot but not smoking. Add the garlic, scallions, lemongrass, red
bell pepper, carrot, snow peas, and shiitakes. Stir-fry for 4 to 5
minutes, until the vegetables are almost done.

5   Add the bean sprouts, corn and tomatoes, if using, hoisin sauce,
soy sauce, and enough broth to make a thin sauce. Add the tofu
and black pepper to taste. Continue stir-frying just until the vegetables are hot. Add the noodles and toss gently until the noodles
and vegetables are hot. Place in a warm serving dish and serve
immediately.

Marinated Tofu and Asparagus Stir-Fry with Noodles

YIELD: 4 MAIN-COURSE SERVINGS

Many vegetable stir-fries can be served over rice or noodles. This sweet-and-hot combination of flavors is particularly well-suited to chewy rice noodles.

8 ounces firm tofu

8 dried shiitake mushrooms

12 ounces thin (1/8-inch) rice stick noodles

2 tablespoons peanut oil

1 teaspoon toasted sesame oil

2 teaspoons minced fresh ginger

1 onion, thinly sliced

1/2 red bell pepper, julienned

2 cups sliced asparagus (cut 1/2-inch thick on the diagonal)

2 cups fresh bean sprouts

Marinade and Sauce

1/4 cup hoisin sauce

2 tablespoons Chinese black or balsamic vinegar

1 tablespoon brown sugar

2 teaspoons chili paste with garlic, or more to taste

1 tablespoon soy sauce

2 tablespoons peanut or canola oil

1   Wrap the tofu in a dish towel and press with a weight to drain off excess water for about 30 minutes (see page 21).

2   In a small bowl, soak the dried mushrooms in warm water for 20 minutes or more.

3   Cover the rice stick noodles with boiling water and set aside for 15 minutes. Drain and rinse in cold water. Cut into 2-inch lengths and set aside to drain in a sieve or colander.

4 To make the marinade, combine the hoisin sauce, vinegar, brown sugar, chili paste, soy sauce, and oil in a small bowl, stirring to dissolve the sugar. Slice the pressed tofu into 3/8-inch-thick slices, then into 3/4-inch squares. Divide the hoisin mixture into 2 portions and pour half the sauce over the tofu, stir gently, and set aside to marinate for at least 15 minutes.

5 Drain and squeeze the mushrooms of excess liquid. Discard the stems and slice the caps 3/8-inch thick.

6 Place a wok or large skillet over high heat for about 30 seconds. Add 1 tablespoon of the peanut oil and the sesame oil, swirl to coat the pan, and heat until hot but not smoking. Add the ginger and stir-fry for 15 seconds. Add the tofu squares and stir-fry for 3 or 4 minutes, until they are lightly crusted. Remove the tofu from the pan and set aside.

7 Add the remaining 1 tablespoon peanut oil to the pan and heat for 30 seconds, stirring any particles loose. Add the onion, red bell pepper, mushrooms, and asparagus and stir-fry for 1 minute. Add the remaining sauce and continue stir-frying until the asparagus is tender crisp, about 2 or 3 minutes.

8 Add the noodles, tofu, and bean sprouts to the wok and gently stir-fry until hot.

NOTE: Instead of combining the stir-fry with the noodles, you can serve the stir-fry over warm noodles. To do so, keep the noodles warm in a covered dish in a 200° F oven. Or, warm the noodles by submerging them in boiling water for 1 minute and then draining.

Broccoli and Mushroom Noodles with Marinated Tofu

YIELD: 4 MAIN-COURSE SERVINGS

In many health food stores and stores that cater to Asian populations, you will find many kinds of tofu. There are variously seasoned, marinated, fried, and baked tofu—each with its own distinctive flavor. This is a good recipe to use to test out these exotic tofu. I usually buy a Thai-marinated tofu or baked smoked tofu.

3/4 pound Chinese egg noodles

1 pound broccoli, florets separated and sliced in half, stems peeled and cut on the diagonal

2 teaspoons cornstarch

3 tablespoons mushroom soy sauce or soy sauce

1/2 cup Garlic Broth (page 219) or vegetable broth (page 218–219)

1 tablespoon toasted sesame oil

1 tablespoon corn or peanut oil

1 tablespoon minced fresh ginger

1 tablespoon minced garlic

1 1/2 teaspoons chili paste with garlic

1 small red bell pepper, cut in 3/8- by 1 1/2-inch strips

4 ounces portobello mushrooms, stems discarded and caps halved and sliced 1/4-inch thick

4 ounces marinated or baked tofu, sliced 1/4 by 1/4 by 1 3/4 inches

Freshly ground black pepper

1 to 2 tablespoons toasted sesame seeds

1 Cook the Chinese egg noodles in a large pot of boiling water until just done, about 5 to 7 minutes. Drain and rinse under cold water. Drain again and hold the noodles in a covered dish in a 200° F oven.

2 Cook the broccoli stems in a large pot of boiling water for about 1 minute. Add the broccoli florets and cook for another 2 minutes,

until the stems are just tender. Drain and plunge in cold water. Drain well and set aside.

3   In a small bowl, combine the cornstarch, soy sauce, and broth. Mix well and set aside.

4   Place a wok or large skillet over high heat for about 30 seconds. Add the sesame and corn or peanut oils, swirl to coat the pan, and heat until hot but not smoking. Add the ginger, garlic, and chili paste and stir-fry until aromatic, about 1 minute. Add the red bell pepper and mushrooms and stir-fry for about 3 minutes. Add the tofu and stir-fry for 1 minute. Add the broccoli and continue stir-frying gently until hot, about 2 minutes. Add the cornstarch mixture and stir-fry until the juices thicken, about 1 minute. Add the black pepper to taste.

5   Pour the stir-fry over the warm noodles in a serving dish and sprinkle with the sesame seeds. Serve hot.

VARIATION: For a spicier dish, substitute 2 red serrano chiles for the red bell pepper and reduce the chili paste with garlic to 1 teaspoon.

Asparagus and Black Bean Sauce over Egg Noodles

YIELD: 4 MAIN-COURSE SERVINGS

Fermented black beans give this dish its distinctive flavor. The salty little morsels add a unique flavor that can't be duplicated by anything else. You'll find them in 8-ounce packages. Don't worry about what to do with the leftover beans—transfer them to an airtight jar away from heat and light and they will keep indefinitely.

12 ounces fresh thin Chinese egg noodles

2 tablespoons peanut oil

1 1/4 pounds asparagus, sliced into 1 1/2-inch lengths

1/2 small red onion, cut vertically into slivers

1/4 pound fresh shiitake mushrooms, stems discarded and caps sliced 1/2-inch thick

Freshly ground black pepper

Sauce

1 tablespoon peanut oil

1 tablespoon minced ginger

2 large garlic cloves, minced

2 scallions, cut in 3/4-inch pieces

2 tablespoons fermented black beans, roughly chopped

1/4 teaspoon red chile flakes

1 cup unsalted vegetable broth (page 218-219)

2 teaspoons cornstarch dissolved in 2 tablespoons vegetable broth

1   Cook the Chinese egg noodles in a large pot of boiling water until just done, about 3 to 4 minutes. Drain and rinse under cold water. Drain well. Place the noodles in a heatproof serving dish and keep warm in a 200° F oven.

2   To make the sauce, heat 1 tablespoon peanut oil in a medium saucepan. Add the ginger, garlic, scallions, black beans, and chile flakes. Sauté over medium-high heat for about 4 minutes, until the scallions have softened. Stir the cornstarch mixture into the

broth and add it to the saucepan. Bring to a simmer and cook for 2 or 3 minutes.

3 Place a wok or large skillet over high heat for 30 seconds. Add the peanut oil, swirl to coat the pan, and heat until hot but not smoking. Add the asparagus, onion, and mushrooms and stir-fry over high heat until the asparagus is tender-crisp, about 3 to 6 minutes. Add the black bean sauce and heat for 1 minute.

4 To serve, pour the asparagus and sauce over the egg noodles. Grind black pepper to taste over the dish and serve hot.

NOTE: My favorite brand of salted fermented black beans is Pearl River Bridge, which comes in a round yellow cardboard box. It looks like a small oatmeal container.

Chinese Broccoli and Black Beans over Brown Noodles

YIELD: 4 MAIN-COURSE SERVINGS

If you haven't been tempted to buy Chinese broccoli before, perhaps this recipe will inspire you. Chinese broccoli, also called gai-lon or gai larn, is a type of Chinese cabbage, very similar to flowering white cabbage. In flavor, Chinese broccoli resembles kale, though it is not at all related. Stems, buds, and leaves can be stir-fried, and the flowers make lovely garnishes.

12 ounces dried thin (1/8-inch) rice stick noodles

2 tablespoons soy sauce

1 pound Chinese broccoli, or substitute broccoli raab

3 tablespoons peanut or canola oil

2 tablespoons minced garlic

2 tablespoons fermented black beans, partly mashed

1 tablespoon oyster sauce

2 teaspoons Chinese black or balsamic vinegar

1/4 cup unsalted vegetable broth (page 218-219)

Freshly ground black pepper

Chili Dipping Sauce (page 211)

1 Cook the rice stick noodles in a large pot of boiling water until just done, about 3 to 5 minutes. Drain and rinse under cold water. Drain again. In a large bowl, combine the noodles with the soy sauce. Toss gently and set aside.

2 Cut the broccoli stems on the diagonal into 1/2-inch pieces. Slice the leaves and florets into 1-inch pieces. Blanch the broccoli in boiling water for 1 minute; plunge into cold water, drain, and set aside.

3 Place a wok or large skillet over high heat for 30 seconds. Add 2 tablespoons of the peanut oil, swirl to coat the pan, and heat until hot but not smoking. Add the noodles and brown them lightly, turning only once or twice. Place the noodles in a serving dish and keep warm in a 200° F oven.

4 Wipe out the pan. Place over high heat for 30 seconds. Add the remaining 1 tablespoon peanut oil, swirl to coat the pan, and heat until hot but not smoking. Add the garlic and the mashed black beans and stir-fry until fragrant, 1 to 2 minutes. Add the oyster sauce, vinegar, and broth and continue stir-frying until the sauce is hot, about 1 minute. Add the Chinese broccoli. Toss gently until the broccoli and bean sauce are hot.

5 To serve, top the warm noodles with the broccoli and bean sauce and grind black pepper over the top. Serve hot with Chili Dipping Sauce passed on the side.

Stir-Fried Chinese Eggplant over Two-Sides Brown

Yield: 4 MAIN-COURSE SERVINGS

The small, slender, light purple Asian eggplants are delightfully tender and mild, but if they are not available, a Western globe eggplant will fill the bill.

Two-Sides-Brown Noodle Cake (page 119)

2 tablespoons peanut oil

1 teaspoon minced ginger

1 teaspoon minced garlic

1/2 small onion, chopped

2 or 3 scallions, green and white parts, cut in 1-inch pieces

3/4 pound unpeeled Asian eggplant (about 3 small eggplant), halved lengthwise and sliced 1/4-inch thick

1/4 pound shiitake or portobello mushrooms, stems removed, caps sliced 3/8-inch thick (about 2 cups)

Sauce

1 1/2 teaspoons cornstarch mixed with 2 teaspoons water

1 teaspoon black bean sauce with chili (preferably Lan Chi brand) or more to taste

1 tablespoon soy sauce

2 tablespoons hoisin sauce

3/4 cup vegetable or chicken broth (pages 218–222)

1   Prepare the noodle cake according to the recipe instructions. Keep warm in a 200° F oven while you prepare the eggplant.

2   Place a wok or large skillet over high heat for about 30 seconds. Add the peanut oil, swirl to coat the pan, and heat until hot but not smoking. Add the ginger, garlic, onion, and scallions and stir-fry over medium high heat for 2 minutes, until softened. Add the eggplant and mushrooms and stir-fry for about 3 minutes, until the eggplant begins to soften.

3   Combine the sauce ingredients and add to the wok. Continue stir-

frying, bringing the mixture to a simmer. Cover and simmer the eggplant for about 10 minutes, adjusting the heat as necessary.

4 To serve, pour the stir-fry over the hot noodle cake and serve immediately.

VARIATION: Add baby zucchini slices, halved cherry tomatoes, or sweet red pepper slices during the last few minutes of cooking.

NOTE: Asian eggplants are often available in specialty markets. The Japanese variety may be purple-black or white in color, while the Chinese variety is sometimes almost lavender in hue with very tender, edible skin. Both types are sweeter than Western globe eggplants, and have fewer seeds and more tender skin.

Grilled Eggplant Stir-Fry

The grilling of the vegetables adds an extra dimension of smokiness and sweet caramelizing that makes all the difference in this dish. A vegetable grill rack is handy for cooking the vegetables, but not necessary if you don't have one. I think of this dish as an Asian ratatouille. It is also delicious served at room temperature.

2 pounds Asian eggplants

2 leeks (1/2 pound)

1 red bell pepper

4 tablespoons peanut oil

12 ounces flat Chinese egg noodles, or fettuccine or linguine

6 large garlic cloves, chopped

Freshly ground black pepper

1 tablespoon toasted sesame seeds (optional)

Garnish: Sprigs of basil leaves (optional)

Sauce

2 teaspoons toasted sesame oil

2 tablespoons rice vinegar

1 tablespoon Asian fish sauce

1 teaspoon sugar

1/2 teaspoon Thai chili paste or chile paste with garlic (preferably Lan Chi brand)

1   Prepare a medium-hot fire in a grill.

2   Prick the eggplants with a fork and slice them in half lengthwise. Trim and wash the leeks and cut the white bulbous part into 2-inch sections, halved lengthwise. Hold the red bell pepper vertically on end, and slice the sides down into sections, discarding the center core with seeds.

3   To make the sauce, combine the sesame oil, rice vinegar, fish sauce, sugar, and chili paste in a medium-size bowl. Set aside.

4 Bring a large pot of water to a boil, add the Chinese egg noodles and cook until just done, about 3 to 4 minutes for fresh noodles, and about 4 to 5 minutes for dried noodles. Drain, rinse with cold water, and drain again. Place the noodles in a covered dish in a 200° F oven to keep warm.

5 Brush the eggplants, leeks, and red bell pepper with 2 tablespoons of the peanut oil and grill them until the flesh is soft, turning frequently, about 4 minutes for the red bell peppers, and about 5 to 7 minutes for the eggplant and leeks, depending on the fire. Remove and slice the eggplant, leeks, and red bell pepper into 1/2-inch pieces.

6 Place a wok or large skillet over high heat for 30 seconds. Add the remaining 2 tablespoons of peanut oil, swirl to coat the pan, and heat until hot but not smoking. Add the garlic and stir-fry for about 45 seconds. Add the eggplant, leeks, red bell pepper, and sauce and continue to stir-fry for about 4 to 5 minutes until the vegetables are fully cooked. Grind black pepper over the stir-fry.

7 Place the warm noodles in individual serving bowls and spoon the eggplant mixture on top. If desired, sprinkle with toasted sesame seeds and garnish with sprigs of basil leaves. Serve at once.

Spicy Seitan, Vegetables, and Noodles with Red Curry Sauce

YIELD: 4 MAIN-COURSE SERVINGS

This spicy hot vegetarian dish has a nice balance of chewy seitan and bright colorful fresh vegetables in a medium-hot coconut curry sauce.

10 ounces fresh Chinese wheat flour noodles

2 1/2 tablespoons peanut oil

1 tablespoon soy sauce

8 ounces seitan, cut in 1/4-inch slices (about 1 1/2 cups)

1 teaspoon minced ginger

2 teaspoons minced garlic

1/2 large onion, sliced into 1/4-inch wedges

2/3 cup red and green bell pepper slices

1 cup broccoli florets

1 small zucchini, sliced in 1/4-inch rounds

1 cup snow peas, large pods sliced in half diagonally

1 (14-ounce) can coconut milk

2 teaspoons Thai red curry paste

1/2 cup canned baby corn (optional)

12 or more Thai or sweet basil leaves, scissored in strips

1 Cook the Chinese wheat flour noodles in a large pot of boiling salted water until just done, about 5 to 7 minutes. Drain and rinse under cold water. Drain again and set aside.

2 Place a wok or large skillet over high heat for 30 seconds. Add 1 1/2 tablespoons peanut oil and the soy sauce, swirl to coat the pan, and heat until hot but not smoking. Add the seitan, ginger, and garlic, and stir-fry for about 3 or 4 minutes until browned. Set aside. Add the remaining 1 tablespoon of oil to the wok and add the onion, bell pepper, broccoli, zucchini, and snow peas and continue stir-frying for 3 or 4 minutes, until the broccoli and snow peas turn bright green.

3 In a small bowl, stir the coconut milk into the red curry paste. Add

the coconut-curry mixture, seitan, baby corn, if using, and basil to the wok and cook for about 5 minutes until the vegetables are tender.

4 Add the noodles to the wok and stir over medium heat until hot. Serve immediately.

NOTE: Seitan is a protein-rich food made from wheat gluten. It is used as meat substitute, particularly in vegetarian cooking in China and Japan. It has a spongy texture and very little taste, but it absorbs flavor very nicely. It is readily found in the refrigerated case in health food stores and Chinese delicatessens or groceries.

Tangerine Noodles

We like these aromatic noodles with asparagus and crisp fried tofu slices, or accompanying a poultry dish.

> 1 pound fresh Chinese wheat flour noodles
>
> 2 teaspoons peanut oil
>
> 1 teaspoon toasted sesame oil
>
> 2 teaspoons tangerine zest or minced dried orange peel
>
> 2 tablespoons chopped scallions
>
> Salt and freshly ground black pepper (optional)

1 Cook the Chinese wheat flour noodles in plenty of boiling water until just done, about 5 to 7 minutes. Drain well.

2 Place a wok or large skillet over high heat for 30 seconds. Add the peanut and sesame oils, swirl to coat the pan, and heat until hot but not smoking. Add the tangerine zest and scallions and stir-fry for about 2 minutes until the scallions begin to soften. Add the noodles and stir-fry until hot. Taste for seasoning. You may wish to add salt or black pepper.

3 Serve immediately or keep warm in a 200° F oven, lightly covered, until serving.

Two-Sides-Brown Noodle Cake

This traditional Cantonese fried noodle cake is crispy on the outside with tender noodles inside. It makes a terrific bed for a stir-fry that comes with its own sauce. A nonstick skillet is the secret to success here.

1/2 pound dried thin Chinese egg noodles (1/16 inch in diameter)

2 teaspoons toasted sesame oil

1/4 cup chopped leek or sweet onion

1/4 cup chopped scallions

1/2 teaspoon salt

About 1/4 cup corn or peanut oil

1   Cook the Chinese egg noodles in a large pot of salted boiling water for 4 or 5 minutes. Drain well and spread out to dry on a large nonstick pan for 10 minutes. Or pat dry with kitchen towels or paper toweling.

2   Put the noodles in a bowl and add the sesame oil, leek, scallions, and salt. Mix the noodles and seasonings together with your fingers.

3   Heat half the oil in a large nonstick skillet over medium-high heat until hot but not smoking. Spread the noodles in the skillet to form an 8- or 9-inch round cake. Press the noodles flat with a spatula. Reduce the heat to medium and cook, covered, until the underside is brown, about 7 minutes or more. Loosen the noodle cake with a spatula and slide it onto a large plate or bread board. Add more oil to the skillet and when hot, turn the noodle cake back into the skillet to brown the other side. Press with a spatula and cook, covered, about 5 to 7 minutes, checking frequently for color. Loosen the noodle cake with a spatula and slide the cake onto a round serving platter or large pie plate.

4   Serve immediately or keep warm in a 200° F oven until serving.

Seafood Noodle Dishes

Mee Krob (SWEET CRISP-FRIED THAI NOODLES)
YIELD: 4 MAIN-COURSE SERVINGS

In Thailand, this is a dish for celebrations—for weddings, births, holidays—and is used as a centerpiece for the feast. Because this dish is very sweet for my taste, I prefer to serve it as part of a multicourse meal featuring several different dishes. Other dishes to serve with this might include Jicama Shrimp Salad on Glass Noodles (page 54), Thai Crab Cakes with Cellophane Noodles (page 142), or Mango Chicken Stir-Fry with Noodles (page 166)—along with stir-fried broccoli or sugar snap peas and a fresh fruit platter.

6 to 8 cups corn or peanut oil for deep-frying

6 ounces dried rice vermicelli

1 tablespoon minced garlic

1/3 cup chopped shallots or onion

2 small red chiles or serrano peppers, julienned

8 ounces boneless, skinless chicken breast, cut in 1/2-inch strips

8 ounces small shrimp, shelled and deveined

3 cups fresh bean sprouts

1/4 cup cilantro leaves

Garnish: Lime wedges and red chiles

Sauce

1/4 cup white sugar

1/4 cup palm or light brown sugar

2 tablespoons fresh lime juice

1 tablespoon white vinegar

2 tablespoons Asian fish sauce

2 tablespoons ketchup

1 tablespoon soy sauce

1 teaspoon grated orange zest

1/2 teaspoon grated lemon zest

1 To make the sauce, combine the white sugar, palm sugar, lime juice, vinegar, fish sauce, ketchup, soy sauce, orange zest, and lemon zest in a small bowl and set aside.

2 Pull the dried rice vermicelli gently apart, breaking them into clumps about 3 inches long. You may wish to do this in a paper bag. Prepare a baking sheet lined with a paper bag and paper towels and lay out a long-handled mesh scooper and slotted spoons to lift the hot noodles out of the oil.

3 In a wok or deep heavy skillet, add oil to a depth of 2 inches. Place a deep-fry thermometer on the edge of the pan. Heat the oil to 375°F. Adjust the heat so the temperature remains stable. Add half the rice sticks to the oil. As soon as they puff up, turn the mass over. Remove the noodles when they have turned a faint golden color and are no longer crackling, about 15 seconds, and transfer them to the lined baking sheet. Repeat with the remaining rice sticks. Keep the noodles warm in a 200°F oven. Remove noodle bits from the oil.

4 Drain and reserve the oil from the wok. Wipe the wok clean. Place the wok over high heat, add 1 tablespoon of oil, swirl to coat the pan, and heat until hot but not smoking. Add the garlic, shallots, chiles and stir-fry until the shallots have softened, about 2 minutes. Add the chicken, and stir-fry until the chicken begins to change color, about 2 minutes. Add the shrimp, and stir-fry until they begin to turn pink and firm. Remove the meat mixture to a plate.

5 Add the sauce ingredients to the wok and cook, stirring constantly until the sauce becomes a glossy syrup, about 5 to 7 minutes. Let cool for about 3 minutes.

6 Add the reserved chicken-shrimp mixture, stir, and add half the noodles. With long-handled spoons or forks, toss gently, separating the clumps while breaking as few noodles as possible. Add the remaining noodles and the bean sprouts, tossing gently to distribute the sauce over all. Heap the noodles onto a serving platter, mounding them into a cone shape. Scatter with cilantro leaves and garnish with the lime wedges and red chiles. Serve while it is still warm and crisp.
NOTE: Look for fairly straight rice vermicelli, loosely packed for this dish. The tightly packed, crinkly noodles are hard to pull apart.

Pad Thai

Pad Thai, a favorite one-dish meal, is eaten by the Thais at any time of day. Street vendors make it rapidly to order in Bangkok and other cities, with regular customers queued up for a snack or meal. I have been in love with this dish for many years and sample it wherever I can. There is no fixed recipe for Pad Thai. There are many variations based on regional style and the makers' preferences. Here is my version, fairly classic, but substituting fresh shrimp for the Thai dried shrimp. Once prepped, the dish comes together very quickly over high heat.

8 ounces dried thin (1/8-inch) rice stick noodles

1 boneless skinless chicken breast (12 to 14 ounces)

3 tablespoons Asian fish sauce

3 tablespoons rice vinegar

1 teaspoon sugar

1 tablespoon rice wine or white wine

2 teaspoons vegetable oil

2 large eggs, beaten

2 tablespoons chopped preserved radish or turnip (available where Asian groceries are sold)

1/4 cup thinly sliced scallions (including some green parts)

3/4 pound shrimp, shelled and deveined

1/2 cup chopped fresh cilantro leaves

2 cups fresh mung bean sprouts

1/3 cup roasted unsalted peanuts, roughly crushed

1/2 teaspoon ground dried chile peppers (available where Asian groceries are sold) or cayenne

Garnish: Lime wedges and cilantro sprigs

1 Break the rice stick noodles into 4- or 5-inch pieces. Cover with boiling water and set aside to soften for 5 minutes. Drain the noodles in a colander.

2 Partially cook the chicken breast in simmering water to cover for 10 minutes, or microwave, covered, for 4 minutes. Shred or cut the chicken into thin pieces.

3 In a small bowl, combine the fish sauce, rice vinegar, sugar, and the rice wine.

4 Prepare and measure the remaining ingredients and have them lined up beside the stove before beginning to stir-fry.

5 Place a wok or large skillet over high heat for 30 seconds. Add the oil, swirl to coat the pan, and heat until hot but not smoking. Add the fish sauce mixture and the eggs, and stir quickly. Immediately add the drained noodles, chicken pieces, preserved radish, and scallions. Stir-fry until the egg coats the noodles, about 1 minute. Add the shrimp and continue stir-frying until the shrimp are pink and cooked through. Add the cilantro, bean sprouts, and half the peanuts, tossing gently until combined.

6 Turn the Pad Thai onto a large serving platter or individual plates and sprinkle lightly with the ground chiles and the remaining crushed peanuts. Garnish with lime wedges and cilantro sprigs. Serve hot.

NOTE: In this recipe, the noodles need only a 5-minute soak in boiling water, since they will cook further with the chicken and shrimp.

Singapore Curry Fried Noodles

Singapore's famous street food is a delight in all its many variations. Frequent additions are barbecued pork, chicken, carrots, Chinese cabbage, hot peppers, and fresh cilantro. In this version, the crispy curried noodles are combined with fresh vegetables and ginger-marinated shrimp. As a street food, the noodles are cooked a serving at a time. To achieve the proper texture in a kitchen with an ordinary stove, you will have to cook the noodles in two batches.

8 ounces dried thin (1/8-inch) rice stick noodles or rice vermicelli

1 pound medium shrimp, peeled and deveined

1/4 cup peanut or corn oil

1 tablespoon curry powder (Madras curry powder is recommended)

1/2 cup chopped shallots

1 tablespoon minced fresh ginger

1/2 cup thinly sliced (about 1/4-inch thick) celery

1 cup julienned scallions (both green and white parts)

1 small red bell pepper, julienned (about 1 cup)

3 cups fresh mung bean sprouts

Freshly ground black pepper

Garnish: Fresh cilantro sprigs

Marinade

1/2 teaspoon toasted sesame oil

1 teaspoon soy sauce

1 tablespoon minced fresh ginger

1 large garlic clove, minced

2 tablespoons rice wine or dry sherry

Sauce

1/3 cup vegetable or chicken broth (pages 218–222)

2 tablespoons soy sauce

1 teaspoon brown sugar

1 To soften the rice noodles, cover them with boiling water and set aside for 15 minutes. Drain.

2 To make the marinade, combine the sesame oil, soy sauce, ginger, garlic, and rice wine in a medium-size bowl. Add the shrimp and stir gently.

3 Combine the sauce ingredients in a small bowl and set aside.

4 Place a wok or large skillet over high heat for 30 seconds. Add 1 tablespoon of the oil, swirl to coat the pan, and heat until hot but not smoking. Add the curry powder and stir for 30 seconds. Add the shallots and ginger. Stir-fry over high heat for 2 to 3 minutes, until the shallots have softened. Remove the shallot mix and set aside.

5 Add another 1 tablespoon of the oil to the wok and reheat until quite hot. Add half the noodles and stir-fry until they are a little bit brown and crispy. Remove the noodles and set aside. Repeat, adding 1 tablespoon of oil to the wok, reheating, and stir-frying the rest of the noodles. Set aside and cover the noodles lightly with foil to keep warm.

6 Reheat the wok and add the remaining 1 tablespoon oil. Add the shrimp, celery, scallions, and red bell pepper. Stir-fry until the shrimp turns pink, about 2 to 3 minutes. Add the shallot mix, the sauce, and the mung bean sprouts.

7 Toss gently. Add the noodles and toss until the noodles are hot. Add black pepper to taste. Serve at once, garnished with cilantro sprigs.

Rice Vermicelli with Shrimp and Scallops

YIELD: 4 MAIN-COURSE SERVINGS

In this dish, the delicious marinade enhances the delicate, sweet flavors of the seafood. The shrimp and scallops are cooked very briefly to retain their freshness.

10 ounces dried rice vermicelli or thin (1/8-inch) rice stick noodles

1/2 pound raw medium shrimp, peeled, deveined, and cut crosswise in half

1/2 pound bay scallops

2 teaspoons minced fresh ginger

1 teaspoon minced garlic

1/4 cup thinly sliced scallions

3 tablespoons mirin

2 teaspoons toasted sesame oil

2 teaspoons fresh lime or lemon juice

2 tablespoons peanut or corn oil

1 small red bell pepper, sliced in 1/4-inch strips

2 cups shredded Napa or Chinese cabbage

1/4 pound sugar snap peas or snow peas, sliced diagonally in 1/2-inch pieces (about 1 1/2 cups)

2 tablespoons soy sauce

1/2 cup vegetable or chicken broth (pages 218–222)

1/4 cup thinly sliced basil leaves or more to taste

Salt and freshly ground black pepper

Garnish: Lime wedges and basil sprigs

1   Cover the rice noodles with boiling water and set aside to soften for 15 minutes. Drain well. Cut the noodles into 2-inch lengths and set aside.

2   In a small bowl, combine the shrimp, scallops, ginger, garlic, scallions, mirin, sesame oil, and lime juice.

3 Place a wok or large skillet over high heat for 30 seconds. Add the oil, swirl to coat the pan, and heat until hot but not smoking. Add the shrimp and scallops. Stir-fry for just a minute or two, until the shrimp begin to turn pink. Scoop the shrimp and scallops out into a small bowl, leaving the juices in the wok.

4 Add the red bell pepper, cabbage, peas, soy sauce, noodles, and broth. Stir-fry until the vegetables have softened and the noodles have absorbed all the broth, about 5 minutes. Add the shrimp, scallops, and basil to the stir-fry. Add salt, black pepper, and fresh basil to taste.

5 Serve hot with wedges of lime and a basil garnish.

Thai Shrimp in Coconut Sauce with Fine Noodles

YIELD: 4 MAIN-COURSE SERVINGS

What could be more enticing than the flavors of shrimp, lemongrass, and basil with a mildly hot coconut sauce. The beautiful pink and red colors of the shrimp and cherry tomatoes are a visual delight.

12 ounces dried thin Chinese egg noodles or angel hair pasta

1 cup coconut milk

1 teaspoon chili paste with garlic or more to taste

1/2 teaspoon ground turmeric

1 tablespoon fresh lime juice

1/4 teaspoon salt

1 tablespoon peanut oil

1 stalk fresh lemongrass, bottom 6 inches minced, or 2 tablespoons frozen minced lemongrass

4 garlic cloves, minced

1 onion, cut in wedges

1 1/2 cups sugar snap peas or snow peas, halved diagonally

1 pound medium raw shrimp, shelled and deveined

1 cup quartered cherry tomatoes or 1 ripe tomato, cubed

1/4 cup chopped basil leaves

2 teaspoons cornstarch dissolved in 2 tablespoons water

1   Cook the noodles in a large pot of boiling water until just done, about 5 minutes. Drain and rinse with cold water. Drain again. Place the noodles in a serving dish, cover, and keep warm in a 200°F oven while you prepare the shrimp.

2   Combine the coconut milk, chili paste, turmeric, lime juice, and salt in a small bowl. Set aside.

3   Place a wok or large skillet over high heat. Add the peanut oil, swirl to coat the pan, and heat until hot but not smoking. Add the lemongrass, garlic, and onion and stir-fry for 3 to 4 minutes, until

the onion has begun to soften. Add the peas and continue stir-frying for 2 minutes until they begin to turn bright green. Add the shrimp, tomatoes, basil leaves, and the coconut milk mixture. Stir gently until the shrimp turn pink, about 2 to 3 minutes. Stir the cornstarch and water mixture and add to the wok to thicken the juices.

4   To serve, pour the shrimp and coconut sauce over the warm noodles and serve at once.

Coconut Prawn Noodles

YIELD: 4 MAIN-COURSE SERVINGS

You can vary the heat of this dish by choosing a milder chile pepper and by adjusting the amount of hot bean sauce you use.

12 ounces dried rice vermicelli or thin (1/8-inch) rice stick noodles

2 tablespoons peanut or canola oil

1 red onion, sliced 1/2-inch wedges

1 tablespoon Asian fish sauce

2 tablespoons chopped fresh cilantro

2 cups mung bean sprouts

Garnish: Lime wedges and cilantro sprigs

Chili Dipping Sauce (page 211)

Sauce

1 3/4 cups coconut milk

3/4 cup firm tofu, cut in small (3/8-inch) cubes

1/2 cup ground pork (about 4 ounces)

2 tablespoons dried shrimp, rinsed with hot water

2 to 3 tablespoons hot bean sauce

2 teaspoons minced fresh red chile, serrano, jalapeño or 1 teaspoon minced Thai bird pepper

1 cup small or medium shrimp, peeled and deveined (about 5 ounces)

3/4 cup diced ripe tomato (optional)

1   Cover the rice noodles with boiling water and set aside to soften for 15 minutes. Drain, rinse with cold water, and rinse again. Scissor into 4-inch lengths and set aside.

2   To make the sauce, heat the coconut milk to a simmer in a medium saucepan. Add the tofu, pork, dried shrimp, hot bean sauce, and chile. Return to a simmer and cook until the pork is tender, about 10 to 15 minutes. Add the shrimp and cook until the

shrimp turns pink, about 2 minutes. Add the diced tomato, if using. Remove from the heat.

3 Heat a wok or large skillet over high heat for 30 seconds. Add the peanut oil, swirl to coat the pan, and heat until hot but not smoking. Add the onion and stir-fry until beginning to brown, about 4 minutes. Add the noodles, fish sauce, and cilantro and continue stir-frying for 2 or 3 minutes. Add the bean sprouts and toss briefly, until the bean sprouts are warm. Remove from the heat.

4 Rewarm the coconut sauce. Place the noodles in a serving dish and pour the sauce over them. Garnish with lime wedges and cilantro sprigs and serve with Chili Dipping Sauce on the side.

NOTE: The tofu breaks down and thickens the sauce as it cooks.

Thai Curried Mussels
and Shrimp

YIELD: 4 MAIN-COURSE SERVINGS

Make sure your mussels are very fresh. If not, double the amount of shrimp, and skip the mussels altogether.

4 ounces dried thin (1/8 inch) rice stick noodles

2 pounds fresh mussels in the shell

3 cups coconut milk

2 tablespoons Homemade Curry Paste (page 224) or a mild yellow curry paste such as Patak's mild curry paste or Daw Sen's curry paste

3 stalks lemongrass, lower half cut in 2-inch pieces (discard the green part)

3 shallots, sliced

3 tablespoons Asian fish sauce

1 tablespoon palm sugar or brown sugar

1/2 teaspoon turmeric powder

1/2 teaspoon salt

6 kaffir lime leaves or 2 teaspoons lime zest

3/4 to 1 pound medium shrimp, peeled and deveined

2 tablespoons fresh lime juice

1 1/2 cups firm ripe tomato wedges

2 red Thai bird peppers or serrano chiles, thinly sliced (optional)

1/2 cup Thai or sweet basil leaves

Garnish: Lime wedges and sprigs of basil

1 Cook the rice stick noodles in a large pot of boiling water until just done, about 3 to 5 minutes. Drain, rinse in cold water, and drain again. Keep the noodles warm in a covered dish in a 200°F oven.

2 Scrub the mussels and remove the beards. Discard any open mussels.

3 Heat a wok or a large covered pan over medium heat. Spoon a few tablespoons of the thicker coconut milk from the top of the can and add to the wok along with the curry paste. Simmer, for a minute or two, stirring. Add the lemongrass, shallots, fish sauce, sugar, turmeric, salt, lime leaves, and the remaining coconut milk. Cook for 2 or 3 minutes until the shallots have begun to soften.

4 Add the mussels to the hot curry. Cover and simmer for 2 or 3 minutes. Add the shrimp. Cover and cook for just a minute or two, until the shrimp have turned pink. Add the lime juice, tomatoes, chiles, and basil leaves and remove from the heat.

5 Place the noodles in a very large warm bowl. Cover with the seafood and hot curry or serve in individual soup bowls. Garnish with lime wedges and sprigs of basil. Serve at once.

NOTE: For adding a richer, more complex flavor to a dish, curry paste is preferable to curry powder. Curry paste is usually oil based and may include chiles, garlic, tamarind, vinegar, and a great number of spices. It keeps indefinitely in the refrigerator.

Gingered Red Curry Scallops

The combination of scallops, citrus juices, and the mild heat of curry are outstanding in this very colorful dish.

1 pound fresh sea scallops

1 tablespoon thinly julienned fresh ginger

1 teaspoon minced garlic

1 teaspoon Thai red curry paste

1/4 cup fresh lime juice

1/4 cup fresh orange juice

2 teaspoons mirin or 1 teaspoon sugar

1/2 teaspoon salt

1 pound fresh Chinese egg noodles or 3/4 pound dried angel hair pasta (cappellini)

1 1/2 tablespoons peanut oil

1/2 cup julienned scallions

1 small red bell pepper, julienned (about 1 cup)

3/4 cup vegetable or chicken broth (pages 218–222)

1   In a medium-size bowl, combine the scallops, ginger, garlic, curry paste, lime juice, orange juice, mirin, and salt. Set aside for 15 to 20 minutes.

2   Cook the noodles in a large pot of boiling water until just done, about 3 to 4 minutes. Drain and rinse with cold water. Drain and set aside.

3   Remove the scallops and the ginger from the marinade. Separate the scallops and pat dry, saving the marinade. Set the ginger aside.

4   Place a wok or large skillet over high heat for 30 seconds. Add 1 tablespoon of the peanut oil, swirl to coat the pan, and heat until hot but not smoking. Add the scallops and cook for about 2 minutes on each side until lightly brown and tender. Remove to a serving dish and cover lightly with foil.

5 Add the remaining 1/2 tablespoon oil to the wok. Heat for 30 seconds, then add the ginger, scallions, and red bell pepper. Stir-fry for 2 or 3 minutes, adding the marinade and some of the broth at intervals until the vegetables are tender-crisp. Remove the vegetables to the serving dish with a slotted spoon and cover lightly with the foil

6 Add the remaining broth to the wok juices. Heat for a minute. Add the noodles to the wok and toss lightly until heated through.

7 To serve, place the noodles and juices in a large serving dish. Top with the scallops and vegetables. Serve immediately.

NOTE: The key to success when cooking scallops is to be sure they enter the pan dry. Don't skip the step of patting them dry. It makes a big difference in texture, allowing the scallops to sear lightly, instead of steaming.

Cilantro Ginger Pesto
with Scallops

YIELD: 4 TO 6 MAIN-COURSE SERVINGS

Taking pesto in its broadest meaning—an herb paste—this pesto has a lovely blend of flavors. It starts with basil and cilantro and gets more punch from plenty of fresh ginger, garlic, and grated lime zest.

12 ounces dried thin Chinese egg noodles or angel hair pasta

1/2 cup chopped scallions

2 cups chopped ripe yellow tomatoes, yellow tomatillos, or cherry tomatoes

1 pound sea scallops, patted dry and sliced in half horizontally

Juice of a lime

Pesto

3 tablespoons chopped fresh ginger

2 large garlic cloves

3/4 cup cilantro leaves

1 1/2 cups Thai or sweet basil leaves

3/4 cup sunflower seeds

2 tablespoons toasted sesame oil

1/2 cup peanut or canola oil

1 1/2 teaspoons finely grated lime zest (zest of 1 large lime)

Salt and freshly ground black pepper

1   To make the pesto, finely chop the ginger and garlic in a food processor fitted with a steel blade. Add the cilantro, basil, and sunflower seeds and process briefly. With the motor running, add the sesame and peanut or canola oils. Add the lime zest and salt and black pepper to taste. Set aside.

2   Cook the noodles in a large pot of boiling water until just done, about 4 to 5 minutes. Drain and place in a large serving bowl. Toss with the pesto, scallions, and tomatoes or tomatillos. Cover with foil to keep warm and set aside.

3 Spray a large nonstick skillet with oil. Heat for about 45 seconds. Add the scallops and sauté for a minute or two, turning to cook both sides. Pour the lime juice over the scallops.

4 To serve, spoon the scallops onto the noodles. Serve at once.

Soba Noodles
with Lime Scallops

YIELD: 4 MAIN-COURSE SERVINGS

The citrus flavors of lime and lemongrass, along with the light heat of the chili paste and ginger, complement the delicate scallops and asparagus.

8 ounces dried soba noodles (plain or green tea)

1 teaspoon peanut or canola oil

1 tablespoon minced fresh ginger

2 teaspoons minced fresh garlic

1 stalk lemongrass, bulb portion sliced diagonally, stem cut into 2-inch lengths, and crushed lightly with the flat side of a knife

1/2 teaspoon chili paste with garlic

1 3/4 cup vegetable or chicken broth (pages 218–222)

2 cups chopped fresh asparagus (3/4-inch pieces)

2 tablespoons Asian fish sauce

1/3 cup fresh lime juice

2 teaspoons mirin or 1 teaspoon sugar

1/2 pound sea scallops, sliced in half horizontally

1/3 cup fresh cilantro leaves, packed

1/4 cup fresh basil leaves, packed

1 Cook the soba noodles in a large pot of salted boiling water over high heat until just done, about 5 to 7 minutes. Drain well. Or, to cook by the *sashimizu* method, bring a large pot of water to a boil. Add the noodles and cook for 2 minutes. Add 1 cup of cold water and return to a boil. Repeat the process twice. Simmer the noodles until tender, about 5 minutes. Drain well.

2 Place a heavy saucepan or casserole over medium heat for 30 seconds. Add the oil, swirl to coat the pan, and heat until hot but not smoking. Add the ginger, garlic, and stem portions of the lemongrass. Stir-fry for about 30 seconds. Add the chili paste and broth. Bring to a boil and simmer, uncovered, for about 8 minutes, until reduced by a third.

3 Steam the asparagus until tender-crisp, about 3 minutes, or micro-wave, covered, for 2 minutes. Plunge into cold water to stop the cooking, then drain.

4 Add the fish sauce, lime juice, mirin, and sliced lemongrass bulb to the reduced broth. Return to a simmer. Remove the lemongrass stems with tongs and add the scallops. Simmer for 2 to 3 minutes, just until the scallops turn white and opaque.

5 Add the cilantro, basil leaves, the asparagus, and the noodles. Taste for sweetness, sourness, and salt and adjust with mirin or sugar, lime juice, and fish sauce. Ladle into bowls and serve hot.

Thai Crab Cakes with Cellophane Noodles

YIELD: 4 MAIN-COURSE SERVINGS

These crab cakes are very pretty, especially if you use a red pepper, with the lacy effect of the fine noodles at the edges of the cakes. They taste best if you use fresh, not frozen, crabmeat.

1 (1.75-ounce) skein cellophane noodles

1 pound fresh lump crabmeat, picked through for shells

1/2 cup minced scallions, green and white parts

2 tablespoons chopped fresh mint

2 tablespoons chopped fresh basil

1 to 2 tablespoons minced hot peppers, jalapeño, serrano, cayenne, or Thai bird peppers

1 tablespoon grated lemon zest

3 tablespoons dry breadcrumbs

1 teaspoon salt

Freshly ground black pepper

2 eggs, beaten

1 to 2 tablespoons corn or peanut oil for frying

Basil Lemongrass Sauce (page 216) or lemon or lime wedges

1 In a small bowl, cover the cellophane noodles with hot tap water and let soak for 15 minutes. Drain, rinse with cold water, and drain again. Scissor the noodles into 3/4-inch lengths.

2 In a large bowl, gently combine the noodles, crabmeat, scallions, mint, basil, hot peppers, lemon zest, breadcrumbs, salt, black pepper to taste, and eggs. Do not over mix; try to retain the crabmeat lumps.

3 Use a rounded tablespoon to form small crab cakes, placing them on waxed paper or plastic wrap. For larger cakes, dip out a scant 1/4 cup and press the crab cake lightly together. Cover with plastic wrap and refrigerate for 30 minutes or more, for ease in handling.

4 Heat a tablespoon of oil in a large nonstick skillet until hot but not smoking. Cook the small crab cakes for about 2 minutes on each side until lightly brown. Larger crab cakes should cook for about 3 minutes per side.

5 Serve hot with Basil Lemongrass Sauce or wedges of lemon or lime.

Lobster Pad Thai

YIELD: 4 MAIN-COURSE SERVINGS

An exotic way to enjoy a luxurious seafood.

1 (2- to 2 1/2-pound) live lobster or 2 cups lobster meat (about 12 ounces)

8 ounces dried thin (1/8-inch) rice noodles

1 fresh red serrano or cayenne chile pepper, seeds removed, minced

3 tablespoons Asian fish sauce

2 tablespoons rice vinegar

1 teaspoon sugar

2 tablespoons chopped preserved radish or turnip (available where Asian foods are sold)

1/4 cup sliced scallions, including some green parts

1 extra-large or 2 medium eggs, beaten

2 cups fresh mung bean sprouts

1/3 cup chopped fresh cilantro leaves

1/3 cup roasted, unsalted peanuts, roughly crushed

Freshly ground black pepper

Garnish: Cilantro sprigs and lime wedges

1 In a very large kettle, bring 3 inches of water to a boil. Plunge the lobster head first into the water and simmer, covered, for 15 minutes. Transfer the lobster to a large platter to cool briefly. When cool enough to handle, remove the meat from the tail and claws and cut into bite-size pieces. Refrigerate the lobster meat, covered with plastic wrap.

2 Break up the noodles into 4-inch lengths. Cover the noodles with boiling water and set aside to soften for 15 minutes. Drain the noodles in a colander.

3 In a small bowl, combine the chile pepper, fish sauce, rice vinegar, sugar, preserved radish, and scallions.

4 Place a wok or large skillet over high heat for 30 seconds. Add the fish sauce mixture and the egg, and stir for 1 minute. Add the drained noodles and stir-fry for 3 to 4 minutes until the noodle-egg mixture is hot. Add the lobster meat, bean sprouts, cilantro, and half the peanuts, tossing gently until combined.

5 Turn the noodles onto a large serving platter or individual plates. Grind fresh pepper over the dish and sprinkle with the remaining peanuts. Serve hot with cilantro sprigs and lime wedges on the side.

NOTE: I think lobsters have better flavor when they are steamed rather than boiled in water to cover. It makes sense to buy a 2- to 2 1/2-pounder. The little lobsters have such a small amount of meat—a 1 1/4 pound lobster has about 1/2 cup meat. The lobster meat may be prepared 1 day ahead and refrigerated.

Stir-Fried Garlic Squid
with **Ramen**

YIELD: 4 MAIN-COURSE SERVINGS

The trick in cooking squid is to do it quickly. It toughens if cooked more than a minute or two. Scoring it on the inside of the body allows it to cook speedily—and makes for a beautiful presentation. Fresh squid has a delicate sweet flavor that blends well with the garlic and crunchy vegetables.

3/4 pound fresh squid, cleaned

1 tablespoon minced fresh ginger

1 tablespoon toasted sesame oil

10.5 ounces ramen noodles (3 small 3.5-ounce packages)

1/4 cup vegetable or chicken broth (pages 218-222)

1 tablespoon rice wine or sherry

1 1/2 tablespoons mushroom soy sauce

1/2 teaspoon sugar

1 teaspoon cornstarch

2 1/2 tablespoons peanut oil

1/4 teaspoon crushed red pepper (optional)

4 garlic cloves, minced

1/2 cup diagonally cut green and white scallion rings (about 3 scallions)

1 small green bell pepper, cut in 3/4-inch squares

1/4 pound button mushrooms, sliced

1 small zucchini, halved and thinly sliced

1/2 cup sliced water chestnuts

Soy Lime Dipping Sauce (page 207) or lime wedges

1 Separate the tentacles of the squid. Cut the squid body in half, lengthwise, and score the inside of the body in a diagonal cross-hatch pattern, being careful not to cut through the squid. Cut the squid body into approximately 1-inch squares.

2 In a medium bowl, combine the ginger and 2 teaspoons of sesame oil. Add the squid and marinate for 20 minutes or more.

3 To a large pot of boiling salted water, add the ramen noodles, and over high heat return to a boil. Cook for 2 minutes. Test; they should be done. Drain and rinse under cold water. Drain and toss with the remaining 1 teaspoon sesame oil. Keep the noodles warm in a covered dish in a 200°F oven.

4 In a small bowl, combine the broth, rice wine, soy sauce, sugar, and cornstarch.

5 Drain the squid and pat dry. Leave the ginger pieces; they add to the flavor.

6 Place a wok or large skillet over high heat for 30 seconds. Add 1 tablespoon of the peanut oil, swirl to coat the pan, and heat until hot but not smoking. Add one-third of the squid and stir-fry for 1 to 2 minutes, just until the pieces curl. Remove the squid to a flat serving dish and stir-fry the next batch, add to the dish in one layer, and then the last batch, keeping the squid in a single layer, so they do not steam.

7 Reheat the wok and add the remaining 1 1/2 tablespoons peanut oil, swirl to coat the pan, and heat until hot but not smoking. Add the crushed red pepper, if using, garlic, and scallion rings. Stir-fry for 1 minute. Add the green bell pepper, mushrooms, zucchini, and water chestnuts and stir-fry until the vegetables are just tender. Add the sauce and toss for a minute until hot. Add the squid and toss very briefly until warm.

8 Serve the squid over the warm noodles with Soy Lime Dipping Sauce or lime wedges.

Tuna with Ginger Sauce on Buckwheat Noodles

YIELD: 4 MAIN-COURSE SERVINGS

This gingery, caramelized sauce is also be good on salmon or bluefish.

8 ounces dried soba noodles

1 teaspoon toasted sesame oil

2 tablespoons minced chives (optional)

2 large scallions, including green parts, minced

1 1/2 tablespoons minced fresh ginger

1 teaspoon minced garlic

1/8 teaspoon red pepper flakes

1 tablespoon mirin

2 tablespoons soy sauce

2 tablespoons hoisin sauce

2 tablespoons peanut or canola oil

2 tablespoons vegetable or chicken broth
(pages 218–222)

4 (6-ounce) tuna steaks

1 Cook the soba noodles in a large pot of salted boiling water over high heat until just done, about 5 to 7 minutes. Drain well. Or, to cook by the *sashimizu* method, bring a large pot of water to a boil. Add the noodles and cook for 2 minutes. Add 1 cup of cold water and return to a boil. Repeat the process twice. Simmer the noodles until tender, about 5 minutes. Drain, rinse under cold water, and drain again.

2 Toss the noodles with the sesame oil, chives, if using, and scallions. Place the noodles in a wide serving dish or platter, cover lightly with foil, and keep warm in a 200°F oven.

3 In a small bowl, stir together the ginger, garlic, red pepper flakes, mirin, soy sauce, hoisin sauce, peanut oil, and chicken broth. Pour the sauce into a large nonstick skillet and bring to a simmer. Add the tuna and simmer for about 3 minutes on each side.

4 To serve, arrange the tuna over the buckwheat noodles on individual plates. Pour the sauce over the tuna. Serve hot.

Salmon with Toasted Sesame Sauce over Chinese Noodles

YIELD: 4 MAIN-COURSE SERVINGS

It's not easy to cook salmon well, with a sauce that complements but does not overwhelm it. The sesame sauce is lovely with the salmon.

1 1/4 pounds center-cut salmon fillet, trimmed and boned

1 recipe Toasted Sesame Sauce (page 212)

1 pound fresh Chinese egg noodles, or 12 ounces dried

1 teaspoon toasted sesame oil

1 1/2 cups snow peas

1 teaspoon cornstarch

1/3 cup vegetable or chicken broth (pages 218–222)

1 1/2 teaspoons hoisin sauce

1 tablespoon peanut oil

1 1/2 tablespoons fresh lemon juice

Garnish: Scallion curls

1   Place the salmon fillet skin side down and with a large sharp knife or cleaver, cut the salmon lengthwise into 2-inch strips, cutting down only as far as the skin. Then, holding the knife at a diagonal slant, cut across the salmon in 3/8-inch-thick slices, sliding the knife off the skin at the bottom of the cut. Place the salmon slices in a shallow bowl or pie plate and cover with the sesame sauce. Refrigerate, covered, for 30 to 60 minutes.

2   Cook the Chinese egg noodles in a large pot of boiling salted water until just done, 1 or 2 minutes for fresh noodles, 4 to 5 minutes for the dried. Drain well and toss the noodles with the sesame oil. Keep the noodles warm in a covered serving dish a 200°F oven.

3   Blanch the snow peas in boiling water for 2 minutes. Drain and plunge into cold water. Drain and set aside.

4   In a measuring cup, combine the cornstarch, broth, and hoisin sauce.

5 Drain the salmon pieces in a large strainer over a bowl, saving the sesame sauce marinade. Heat a large nonstick skillet or wok over high heat for 30 seconds. Add the peanut oil, swirl to coat the pan, and heat until hot but not smoking. In two batches, cook the salmon for about 2 minutes per side, until barely done, transferring the slices to the noodles in the serving dish as they are cooked.

6 Reheat the skillet and add the sesame sauce marinade. Heat to a simmer. Stirring constantly, add the broth mixture. Cook for a minute and add the lemon juice. Taste for seasoning and pour the sauce over the salmon. Serve at once, garnished with the scallion curls.

Noodles with Chicken and Duck

Red Curry Chicken
with Noodles

You control the heat by adding more or completely omitting the hot chili sauce. The homemade Chili Dipping Sauce (page 211) goes well in this dish as does any sweet and hot Thai chili sauce.

8 ounces dried rice vermicelli

1 tablespoon peanut oil

1 tablespoon Thai red curry paste

3 medium shallots, chopped (1/4 cup)

10 ounces boneless chicken breasts or thighs, sliced into 1/2- by 3-inch strips

2 tablespoons Asian fish sauce

1 teaspoon hot chili sauce or more to taste (optional)

2 tablespoons water

1/2 cup halved and thinly sliced red onion

2 tablespoons fresh lime juice

1/2 cup chopped cilantro leaves

Garnish: Lime wedges

Topping

1 tablespoon peanut oil

1 serrano, jalapeño, or Thai bird pepper, finely chopped

3 garlic cloves, halved and sliced thin

1/2 cup roasted unsalted peanuts

1   Cover the rice vermicelli with boiling water and set aside to soften for 15 minutes. Drain and rinse in cold water. Leave draining in a sieve or colander.

2   To make the topping, heat a wok or large skillet over high heat for 30 seconds. Add 1 tablespoon of peanut oil, swirl to coat the pan, and heat until hot but not smoking. Add the chile pepper, garlic, and peanuts. Stir-fry for about 2 minutes over medium heat until

the peanuts have toasted light brown and the garlic is golden. Be careful not to burn the garlic. Set aside.

3 Heat the wok for 15 seconds. Add the peanut oil, swirl to coat the pan, and heat until hot but not smoking. Add the red curry paste and stir for 1 minute. Add the shallots and stir-fry for 2 minutes. Add the chicken and stir-fry until the pieces have whitened, about 3 minutes. Add the fish sauce, hot chili sauce, if using, and water. Bring to a simmer for a minute or two until the chicken is cooked.

4 Add the drained noodles, onion, lime juice, and half the cilantro. Stir-fry and toss the noodles and chicken until thoroughly hot.

5 Turn onto a serving dish and sprinkle with the peanut topping and remaining cilantro. Serve at once with lime wedges on the side.

Curried Coconut Noodles
with Chicken

YIELD: 4 TO 6 MAIN-COURSE SERVINGS

I like to make the sauce ahead for this dish. If all the ingredients are measured out, and the noodles are soaked, it is easy to put it together in a few minutes.

12 ounces thin (1/8-inch) rice stick noodles

2 tablespoons peanut oil

1 large onion, roughly chopped

1 1/2 tablespoons minced garlic

2 tablespoons minced fresh ginger

1 teaspoon ground cumin

1 teaspoon crushed red pepper flakes

1 teaspoon ground turmeric

1/2 teaspoon salt

1 teaspoon freshly ground black pepper

2 cups peeled, seeded, and chopped fresh or canned tomatoes

1 3/4 cups fresh coconut milk or 1 (14-ounce) can coconut milk

1/4 cup fresh lime juice

2 boneless, skinless chicken breasts, cut in approximately 1- by 2-inch strips

2 cups fresh mung bean sprouts

1 cup fresh basil leaves, large leaves torn in half

Garnish: Lime wedges and basil sprigs

1 Cover the rice stick noodles with boiling water and set aside to soften for 15 minutes. Drain, rinse in cold water, and drain again. Set aside.

2 Place a large wok or skillet over high heat for 30 seconds. Add 1 tablespoon of the peanut oil, swirl to coat the pan, and heat until hot but not smoking. Add the onion and garlic, and stir-fry until softened, about 4 minutes. Add the ginger, cumin, red pepper

flakes, turmeric, salt, and black pepper. Continue stir-frying for 2 or 3 minutes, until aromatic. Add the tomatoes, coconut milk, and lime juice. Simmer until the sauce begins to thicken, about 10 minutes. Add the noodles and stir until they are coated with the sauce. Turn them into a serving dish.

3 Wipe out the wok or skillet. Heat over high heat for 30 seconds; add the remaining tablespoon of oil, swirl to coat the pan, and heat until hot but not smoking. Add the chicken and stir-fry until the chicken is tender, about 4 minutes. Add the noodles, bean sprouts, and basil leaves, and heat, stirring gently, until hot. Serve immediately, garnished with lime wedges and sprigs of basil.

Asian Pesto Noodles
with Chicken
YIELD: 4 MAIN-COURSE SERVINGS

A cilantro-based pesto transforms this Italian-style dish into a Pacific Rim noodle dish.

> 2 boneless, skinless chicken breast halves
>
> 3/4 pound ramen, Chinese wheat flour, or fettuccine noodles
>
> 1 recipe Asian Pesto Sauce (page 214)
>
> Garnish: Cilantro or basil sprigs

1   Bring a medium-size pot of salted water to a boil. Add the chicken breasts, return the water to a boil, then reduce the heat to keep the water at a simmer. Cook for 15 minutes. Turn off the heat, cover the pot, and let the chicken stay in the water for 30 minutes. Remove the chicken from the pot and reserve the broth for another use. Cut the chicken into 3/4-inch chunks and set aside.

2   To a large pot of salted boiling water, add the noodles and over high heat return to a boil. Cook the noodles until just done, about 3 to 4 minutes for ramen noodles, 5 to 7 minutes for wheat flour noodles, and 9 to 11 minutes for the fettuccine. Drain.

3   Toss the noodles with the chicken and Asian Pesto Sauce. Garnish with cilantro or basil sprigs. Serve warm.

Pancit Bihon with Chicken and Shrimp
YIELD: 4 MAIN-COURSE OR 6 TO 8 FIRST-COURSE SERVINGS

Pancit Bihon refers to rice noodles. This is a braised noodle dish with meats and vegetables is served all over the Philippines, usually as snack food. Noodles were originally brought to the Philippines by the Chinese and were widely adapted and adopted.

8 ounces dried rice vermicelli

1 tablespoon peanut or canola oil

1/2 pound boneless, skinless chicken, sliced into thin strips

1 cup chopped onion

2 garlic cloves, chopped

1/2 cup julienned carrot

2 cups thinly sliced cabbage

2 tablespoons mushroom soy sauce or soy sauce

1 tablespoon Asian fish sauce (optional)

1/4 pound medium peeled raw shrimp (1 cup)

1 cup chicken broth (page 220–222)

1/2 teaspoon freshly ground black pepper

Garnish: Lime wedges

1   Cover the rice vermicelli with boiling water and set aside to soften for 15 minutes. Drain, rinse with cold water. Scissor into 4-inch lengths and set aside.

2   Heat a wok or large skillet over high heat for 30 seconds. Add the oil, swirl to coat the pan, and heat until hot but not smoking. Add the chicken and stir-fry for 2 to 3 minutes. Add the onion, garlic, and carrot, and stir-fry until the vegetables begin to soften, about 3 minutes. Add the cabbage, soy sauce, and fish sauce, if using. Stir-fry for 2 minutes, until the cabbage is wilted. Add the shrimp and cook for 1 minute, until simmering. Add the noodles, chicken broth, and black pepper. Simmer, stirring frequently, until the vegetables are tender and the dish has absorbed most of the broth, about 4 to 5 minutes.

3   Serve hot, garnished with lime wedges.

Mirin Chicken
with Ramen Noodles

A sweet marinade on the chicken becomes a lovely seared crust—and a crunchy contrast to the soft noodles.

1/3 cup mirin

1/3 cup soy sauce

1/3 cup chicken broth (page 220–222)

1 teaspoon sugar

4 boneless, skinless chicken breast halves

1/2 ounce dried black fungus (about 1/4 cup)

6 cups Dashi (page 215 or made from dashi concentrate

7 ounces ramen noodles

2 scallions, very thinly sliced

Accompaniments: Freshly grated ginger, julienned daikon radish, soy sauce, Hot Chili Oil (page 223)

1 In a small saucepan, bring the mirin to a simmer and reduce by half, about 4 minutes. Remove from the heat and add the soy sauce, chicken broth, and sugar. Stir well. Add the chicken and marinate in this mixture for 45 minutes.

2 In a small bowl, soak the dried black fungus in cold water for 30 minutes. Drain.

3 In a large pot, bring the dashi to a boil. Add the ramen noodles and cook for 2 to 3 minutes. Drain the noodles, reserving the broth. Cover the noodles lightly with foil. Leave the dashi broth in the pan.

4 Heat a large nonstick skillet or wok over high heat until very hot. Drain the chicken breasts and place in the hot skillet. Press flat with a spatula and sear to a dark brown on one side, about 4 minutes. Turn and sear the other side, for 2 minutes. Remove the chicken breasts to a cutting board and let stand for 5 or 10 minutes. Meanwhile, reheat the dashi broth.

5 Place the noodles in individual bowls. Distribute the scallions and black fungus among the bowls. Pour the dashi broth over the noodles. Slice the chicken breasts and place 5 or 6 slices, upright and close together, on each bowl of noodles. Serve at once, accompanied by small dishes of grated ginger, julienned daikon, soy sauce, and hot chili oil.

NOTE: Ramen noodle packets are handy to have on hand, but I prefer discarding the seasonings with them, in favor of my own. The nonstick skillet is preferable to a wok in this recipe; the flat surface makes it easier to flatten the breasts and get a nice seared crust on them.

Soba Noodles with Chicken, Mushrooms, and Snow Peas

YIELD: 4 MAIN-COURSE SERVINGS

In this recipe the chicken and mushroom sauce cooks in one pan and the noodles and snow peas in another. Combined at the end, it is a fairly quick meal to make.

2 tablespoons hoisin sauce

2 tablespoon rice vinegar

1 1/2 cups chicken broth (pages 220–222)

1/2 teaspoon salt

1/2 tablespoon freshly ground black pepper

1 tablespoon toasted sesame oil

1 tablespoon cornstarch

1 tablespoon peanut oil

1 tablespoon minced fresh ginger

1 teaspoon minced garlic

10 ounces boneless chicken breast or thighs, cut in 1/2- by 3-inch strips

1/2 pound mixed fresh mushrooms (crimini, button mushrooms, or shiitake caps), sliced

3/4 pound soba noodles or rice vermicelli

3 cups snow peas (about 8 ounces)

1 In a small bowl, combine the hoisin sauce, rice vinegar, 3/4 cup chicken broth, salt, and black pepper. Set aside.

2 In a small bowl, combine the toasted sesame oil, the remaining 3/4 cup chicken broth, and the cornstarch. Set aside.

3 Place a wok or large skillet over high heat for 30 seconds. Add the peanut oil, swirl to coat the pan, and heat until hot but not smoking. Add the ginger and garlic and stir-fry for 1 minute. Add the chicken and stir-fry until the chicken has whitened, about 2 minutes. Push the chicken to one side of the wok.

4 Add the mushrooms and the hoisin sauce mixture. Stir-fry over

162

medium-high heat until the mushrooms have begun to soften, about 6 minutes. Combine the mushrooms and the chicken in the wok and add the sesame oil mixture. Continue to stir-fry until the chicken and mushrooms are tender, about 3 to 4 minutes.

5 At the same time, in a large pot of salted boiling water, cook the soba noodles and the snow peas together, until the noodles are just cooked, about 3 to 5 minutes. Drain.

6 Combine the noodles and snow peas with the chicken-mushroom sauce and serve immediately.

Tamarind Chicken
with Buckwheat Noodles

This dish is sweet and hot, enlivened still further by the fresh ginger.

1/4 cup tamarind purée (pages 16-17)

2 teaspoons minced fresh ginger

2 tablespoons soy sauce

1 tablespoons sugar

1/3 cup chicken or vegetable broth (pages 218–222)

6 chicken thighs, skin removed

12 ounces soba noodles

2 teaspoons toasted sesame oil

1 small onion, vertically sliced

1/3 cup julienned red bell pepper

1/4 teaspoon crushed red pepper flakes

1 In a small saucepan, bring the tamarind purée, ginger, soy sauce, sugar, and broth to a simmer, stirring to dissolve the sugar. Remove from the heat and cool slightly. Add the chicken and marinate in this mixture for 45 minutes or longer.

2 To a large pot of boiling salted water, add the soba noodles, and over high heat return to a boil. Cook for 5 to 7 minutes until the noodles are just cooked. Drain and rinse under cold water. Drain again and toss the noodles with sesame oil. Keep the noodles warm in a covered dish in a 200°F oven.

3 Heat a large nonstick skillet over high heat until very hot. Drain the chicken thighs, reserving the marinade, and place the chicken in the hot skillet. Sear to a dark brown on one side, about 3 minutes. Turn and sear the other side, for 2 minutes. Add the marinade, onion, and red bell pepper. Simmer, covered, until the chicken is tender, adding a little water if needed. This will take about 6 to 8 minutes. Remove the chicken to a cutting board and bone the pieces, cutting them into strips. Return the chicken to the

skillet. Add the red pepper flakes and simmer until tender, about 3 minutes. Taste for seasoning.

4 Serve the chicken over the warm noodles.

NOTE: In this recipe, I like the darker thigh meat with the sweet and sour, spicy tamarind sauce. Fresh portobello or shiitake mushrooms would be a good addition.

Mango Chicken Stir-Fry
with Noodles

YIELD: 4 MAIN-COURSE SERVINGS

Mango adds a lush, tropical note to this sweet-spicy noodle dish.

2 tablespoons mushroom soy sauce or soy sauce

1 tablespoon oyster sauce

1 teaspoon cornstarch

1 pound boneless chicken, cut into 3/4-inch cubes

12 ounces fresh Chinese egg noodles

2 teaspoons toasted sesame oil

1 tablespoon peanut oil

2 teaspoons minced fresh ginger

1/2 red serrano chile, julienned

1/2 cup julienned red bell pepper

3 large scallions, diagonally sliced (about 2/3 cup)

2 cups ripe 1-inch cubed mango or frozen mango cubes

2/3 cup julienned water chestnuts

2 tablespoons lemon juice

1 In a medium bowl, combine the soy sauce, oyster sauce and cornstarch. Add the chicken, stir to coat, and set aside for a few
minutes.

2 To a large pot of boiling salted water, add the Chinese egg noodles,
and over high heat return to a boil. Test the noodles at this point.
They should be done. Drain and rinse in cold water. Drain well
and toss with 1 teaspoon of the sesame oil. Keep the noodles warm
in a covered dish in a 200°F. oven.

3 Place a wok or large skillet over high heat for 30 seconds. Add the
remaining 1 teaspoon sesame oil and the peanut oil, swirl to coat
the pan, and heat until hot but not smoking. Add the ginger, and
stir-fry for 15 seconds; add the chicken and stir-fry for 4 minutes,
until the chicken is partially cooked. Add the chile, red bell pepper,
scallions, and mango. Stir-fry for 2 or 3 minutes, until softened.

Add the water chestnuts and lemon juice. Continue stir-frying for 2 minutes, until the chicken and vegetables are tender. Taste for seasoning.

4 Serve the chicken over the warm noodles.

NOTE: I have located frozen mango at my local health food store and keep it on hand, now. It is very versatile and has excellent flavor.

Chicken, Chinese Mushrooms, and Asparagus Stir-Fry

YIELD: 4 MAIN-COURSE SERVINGS

The spicy hoisin-flavored mushrooms retain their firm chewiness in this stir-fry, providing a nice balance in texture to the meaty chicken and crunchy asparagus.

1 ounce small dried shiitake mushroom caps

2 tablespoons hoisin sauce

1 tablespoon Chinese black vinegar

1 tablespoon rice wine or dry sherry

1 large garlic clove, minced

1 teaspoon minced fresh ginger

2 whole star anise

12 ounces dried Chinese egg noodles

2 teaspoons toasted sesame oil

1/3 cup chicken broth (pages 220–222)

2 tablespoons soy sauce

2 teaspoons cornstarch

1 tablespoon peanut oil

1 1/4 pounds boneless, skinless chicken breast, cut in 1-inch pieces

Freshly ground pepper to taste (1/8 teaspoon or more)

3 cups 1-inch asparagus pieces (about 12 ounces)

2 scallions, cut in 1-inch pieces

1   In a small bowl, soak the dried mushrooms in hot water for 20 to 30 minutes until soft. Squeeze the moisture from the mushrooms.

2   In a small saucepan, combine the hoisin sauce, vinegar, rice wine, garlic, ginger, star anise, and the mushroom caps. Simmer, stirring frequently, until the mushrooms have absorbed most of the sauce, about 15 minutes. Set aside.

3   To a large pot of boiling salted water, add the Chinese egg noodles, and over high heat, return to a boil. Cook the noodles until tender

but still firm, about 4 to 5 minutes. Drain and rinse with cold water. Toss the noodles with sesame oil. Keep the noodles warm in a covered dish in a 200°F oven.

4 In a measuring cup, combine the chicken broth, soy sauce, and cornstarch. Remove the star anise from the mushrooms.

5 Place a wok or large skillet over high heat for 30 seconds. Add the peanut oil, swirl to coat the pan, and heat until hot but not smoking. Add the chicken and mushrooms, with their marinade, and stir-fry over high heat for 4 minutes. Grind some black pepper over the chicken as you stir-fry. Push the chicken and mushrooms to one side of the wok. Add the asparagus and scallions and stir-fry for 2 minutes. Add the cornstarch mixture to the asparagus and simmer until the sauce thickens slightly, about 1 minute. Toss the chicken, asparagus, and mushrooms together and simmer for a minute until hot.

6 Serve the stir-fry over the warm noodles.

Chicken and Eggplant Stir-Fry

YIELD: 4 MAIN-COURSE SERVINGS

It is worth hunting down Asian eggplants for this dish. They are sweet, tender, and almost seedless—a delight to cook with—and the dish is not quite the same without them. By parboiling the eggplant, you can cut down on the amount of oil needed to cook this vegetable which absorbs oil like a sponge.

2 tablespoons mushroom soy sauce or soy sauce

1/4 cup oyster sauce

1 teaspoon sugar

1/2 teaspoon cornstarch

1 pound boneless, skinless chicken breast or thighs, cut into 3/4-inch cubes

12 ounces dried Chinese wheat flour or fettuccine noodles

3 teaspoons toasted sesame oil

1 1/2 pounds Chinese or Japanese eggplant, quartered lengthwise, cut into 1 1/2-inch pieces

1 tablespoon peanut oil

1 teaspoon seeded and finely minced Thai chiles or serrano chiles

1 tablespoon chopped garlic

2/3 cup sliced leeks or chopped shallots

1/2 cup vegetable or chicken broth (pages 218–222)

1/4 cup chopped fresh Thai or sweet basil leaves

Garnish: Basil sprigs

1 In a medium bowl, combine the soy sauce, 1 tablespoon of the oyster sauce, the sugar, and cornstarch. Stir to combine and add the chicken. Set aside to marinate.

2 To a large pot of salted boiling water, add the noodles, and over high heat return to a boil. Cook the noodles until just done, about 5 to 7 minutes for wheat flour noodles and 9 to 11 minutes for the fettuccine. Drain and rinse in cold water. Drain and toss with 1

tablespoon of the toasted sesame oil. Hold the noodles, covered, in a 200°F oven.

3 To a large pot of salted boiling water, add the eggplant. Simmer for 3 minutes, until the eggplant skin starts to change color. The eggplant cubes will still hold their shape. Drain the eggplant and set aside.

4 Place a wok or large skillet over high heat for 30 seconds. Add the peanut oil and remaining 2 tablespoons sesame oil, swirl to coat the pan, and heat until very hot but not smoking. Add the chiles and garlic; stir-fry for 10 seconds. Add the chicken and stir-fry for 4 minutes, until the chicken is partially cooked. Add the shallots, broth, and remaining 3 tablespoons oyster sauce and stir-fry for 1 minute. Add the eggplant and stir-fry for 2 minutes, until the eggplant has softened and is tender. Add the basil and toss gently.

5 Serve the eggplant and chicken over the warm noodles garnished with sprigs of basil.

Grilled Lemongrass Chicken with Cilantro Noodles

YIELD: 4 MAIN-COURSE SERVINGS

Lemongrass has such a lovely flavor—there's nothing like it!

12 ounces dried rice vermicelli

4 stalks lemongrass, trimmed and minced or 1/2 cup frozen minced lemongrass

2 garlic cloves

2 tablespoons sugar

1 1/2 tablespoons chopped fresh ginger

1 fresh red Thai, serrano, or jalapeño chile, seeded and minced

2 tablespoons peanut oil

2 teaspoons toasted sesame oil

1/4 cup Asian fish sauce

1/3 cup fresh lime juice

1 pound boneless chicken breasts or thighs, cut into 1-inch pieces

1 red onion, 1/2 cut in 1-inch pieces, and 1/2 quartered and finely sliced (about 1/2 cup)

1/4 cup water

1/2 cup chopped fresh cilantro

1/2 cup crushed roasted peanuts

Garnish: Cilantro sprigs

1 Cook the rice vermicelli in a large pot of boiling water until just done, about 3 to 5 minutes. Rinse well in cold water and set aside in a sieve or colander to drain.

2 In a mini processor or blender, combine the lemongrass, garlic, sugar, ginger, chile, peanut oil, sesame oil, fish sauce, and lime juice. Blend to a paste, scraping down the sides.

3 Prepare a medium hot fire in the grill.

4   In a nonreactive bowl or plastic zippered bag, combine the chicken with 1/4 cup of lemongrass mixture and toss to coat. Set aside to marinate for 20 minutes or more. While the chicken marinates, soak 8 bamboo skewers in water for 20 minutes or more. Thread the chicken onto skewers alternating with pieces of red onion.

5   Add the water, sliced red onion, and cilantro to the remaining lemongrass mixture. Toss the rice noodles with the lemongrass mixture and the peanuts.

6   Grill the chicken skewers until the chicken is done, 4 to 5 minutes, turning once.

7   Serve the hot chicken skewers over the room-temperature noodles, garnished with cilantro sprigs.

NOTE: This would be an excellent hot weather dish to prepare ahead for entertaining. And, of course, the heat of the marinade could be increased. If you don't want to grill, the chicken can be broiled instead.

Green Glass Noodle-Stuffed Chicken Breasts

YIELD: 6 MAIN-COURSE SERVINGS

I like to start this recipe early, by making the filling and chilling it. It is much easier to stuff the breasts when the filling is cold and firm. This recipe takes a bit of time, but it is a great dinner party meal that can all be done ahead, with the final baking prepared just before dining.

1 (1.75-ounce) skein cellophane noodles

3 large boneless skinless chicken breasts

2 garlic cloves

2 scallions

1/2 cup water chestnuts or cubed jicama

1/2 cup lemon basil, Thai hairy basil, or sweet basil leaves

2 tablespoons cilantro leaves

1 tablespoon mint leaves (optional)

3 tablespoons fresh lemon or lime juice

1 teaspoon toasted sesame oil

1 egg yolk

1/4 teaspoon salt

Freshly ground black pepper

2 tablespoons vegetable oil

Basil Lemongrass Sauce (page 216) or Southeast Asian Sweet and Sour Sauce (page 209)

1 In a small bowl, cover the cellophane noodles with hot tap water and set aside to soften for 10 to 15 minutes. Drain and cut into 2-inch lengths. Set aside.

2 Split the chicken breasts in half and remove the center cartilage. Separate the strip (chicken tender) from the inside of each breast half. Between sheets of waxed paper, pound the chicken breast to an even thickness of about 1/4 inch and set aside.

3 With the food processor running, drop the garlic cloves through the feed tube and mince. Add the scallions, including half the

green parts, and the water chestnuts and process briefly to a fine chop. Remove to a bowl.

4 In a small bowl, combine the basil, cilantro, and mint leaves, if using, with the lemon juice. Place these in the food processor and pulse briefly. Add these herbs to the scallion-water chestnut mixture.

5 Place 3 of the chicken tenders in the food processor with the toasted sesame oil, egg yolk, salt, and black pepper, and pulse very briefly into small chunks. Add the chicken and glass noodles to the other ingredients and mix gently with a fork. Chill the filling for 1 hour. (The remaining 3 chicken tenders may be baked with the dish, or frozen for another use.)

6 On each pounded chicken breast, spread a layer of chicken- noodle filling, spreading it evenly and leaving a 1/2 inch of breast uncovered at the side. Roll up the chicken breast, using toothpicks to close the breast on the uncovered side.

7 Heat the oil in a large skillet and brown the filled breasts on both sides, seam side down first, for about 2 minutes on each side. Place them close together in an oiled ovenproof serving dish. (The dish may be refrigerated at this point and baked later.)

8 Preheat the oven to 350°F. Bake, uncovered, for 20 to 25 minutes. Remove and let stand for 5 minutes.

9 Remove the toothpicks before slicing the chicken 3/4-inch thick. Serve hot with Basil Lemongrass Sauce or Southeast Asian Sweet and Sour Sauce.

NOTE: If you don't have a meat mallet to flatten the chicken breasts, try using a small cast-iron skillet.

Stir-Fried Fragrant Duck over Tangerine Noodles

YIELD: 4 MAIN-COURSE SERVINGS

Succulent duck slices over Tangerine Noodles need just a lightly steamed green vegetable, such as sugar snap peas or Chinese broccoli, for a delightful meal.

2 boneless skinless duck breasts

Tangerine Noodles (page 118)

1 tablespoon peanut oil

3 whole scallions, cut in 1-inch pieces

1 small red bell pepper, cut in 3/4-inch square pieces (about 1 cup)

1/4 pound fresh shiitake mushrooms, stems removed, caps sliced 3/8 inch

Marinade

1 tablespoon rice wine or dry sherry

2 teaspoons toasted sesame oil

2 teaspoons hot chili oil

1 tablespoon minced fresh ginger

3 star anise

2 teaspoons grated orange or tangerine peel, white pith removed, or julienned dried orange peel

Sauce

2 tablespoons soy sauce

2 tablespoons hoisin sauce

1 tablespoon honey

Juice of 2 oranges or tangerines

1 tablespoon cornstarch mixed with 1 tablespoon water

1 Halve the duck breasts and cut across into thin slices, about 3/8-inch thick.

2 To make the marinade, combine the rice wine, toasted sesame oil, hot chili oil, ginger, star anise, and orange peel in a nonreactive bowl. Add the duck and marinate for 30 minutes or more.

3 Prepare the noodles according to the recipe directions. Keep warm in a covered serving dish in a 200°F oven when you cook the duck.

4 To make the sauce, combine the soy sauce, hoisin sauce, honey, orange juice, and cornstarch and water in a small bowl. Set aside.

5 Heat a wok or large skillet over high heat for 30 seconds. Add the peanut oil, swirl to coat the pan, and heat until hot but not smoking. Add half the duck slices and stir-fry for 2 to 3 minutes, until the duck is cooked rare. Remove and keep warm. Reheat the wok, adding a little more oil if needed. Stir-fry the remaining duck slices until cooked rare and add to the rest of the duck.

6 Add the scallions, red bell pepper, and mushrooms to the wok and stir-fry for 3 to 4 minutes, until slightly softened. Add the sauce to the wok and cook, stirring, until the sauce thickens. Add the duck slices to the sauce and bring to a simmer.

7 Spoon the duck and sauce over the Tangerine Noodles and serve at once.

VARIATION: Substitute Two-Sides-Brown Noodle Cake (page 119) for the Tangerine Noodles.

Hearty Beef and Pork Dishes

Ants Climbing a Tree

4 MAIN-COURSE SERVINGS

Small bits of pork (the ants) swarm over transparent cellophane noodles (the tree branches) in this whimsically named Sichuan classic. It is usually made quite spicy, but my version is somewhat mild.

5 or 6 dried shiitake mushrooms

3 (1.75-ounce) skeins cellophane noodles

2 tablespoons soy sauce

1 tablespoon rice wine or dry sherry

2 teaspoons cornstarch

1/2 pound boneless pork, chopped

3 tablespoons peanut oil

2 teaspoons toasted sesame oil

1 1/2 tablespoons minced fresh ginger

1/2 cup thinly sliced scallion, both green and white parts

2 to 3 teaspoons Chinese chili sauce or hot bean sauce

1/3 cup mushroom soaking liquid

1/2 cup vegetable or chicken broth (pages 218–222)

1   Soak the mushrooms in 3/4 cup hot water until softened, 20 to 30 minutes. Squeeze the excess liquid from the mushrooms, saving 1/3 cup of the soaking liquid. Discard the stems, and cut the caps into a 1/2-inch dice.

2   Cover the cellophane noodles with hot tap water and set aside to soften for 15 minutes. Drain, rinse in cold water, and drain again. Scissor the noodles into 5-inch lengths.

3   Blend the soy sauce, rice wine, and cornstarch in a food processor fitted with a steel blade. Add the pork and pulse a few times, until you have small pieces. Or, chop or grind the pork into small bits and combine with the soy sauce, rice wine, and cornstarch.

4   Heat a wok or large skillet over high heat for 30 seconds. Add the peanut and sesame oils, swirl to coat the pan, and heat until hot

but not smoking. Add the ginger, scallion, and chili sauce and stir-fry for about 1 minute. Add the pork. Stir-fry vigorously, breaking up the pork into small bits, until no pink meat remains.

5 Add the mushroom liquid and the broth and return to a simmer. Add the noodles and stir to combine. Simmer gently, until the liquid has cooked down and the noodles have absorbed the juices, about 3 minutes. Taste for seasoning. Serve hot.

Dan-Dan Noodles

YIELD: 4 MAIN-COURSE SERVINGS

Noodles are, of course, the ultimate street food. The dish gets its name from the peddlers' pails banging together as they wend their way through the streets. Feel free to adjust the heat of the hot chili sauce or oil to your preference.

9 ounces ground pork

1 tablespoon minced fresh ginger

2 tablespoons toasted sesame oil

1 pound fresh lo mein noodles

1 tablespoon peanut oil

1 tablespoon minced garlic

1/2 cup chopped scallions, both white and green parts

4 cups chopped Napa cabbage

Garnish: Crushed dry-roasted peanuts (about 1 tablespoon)

Sauce

3 tablespoons Asian sesame paste

1 to 2 tablespoons Chinese hot chili sauce or Hot Chili Oil (page 223)

2 tablespoons soy sauce

1/3 cup vegetable or chicken broth (pages 218–222)

1 tablespoon brown sugar

1 tablespoon rice vinegar

1 In a small bowl, combine the ground pork, ginger, and toasted sesame oil. Cover and set aside.

2 Cook the lo mein noodles in a large pot of boiling water until tender but still firm, about 5 to 7 minutes. Drain and rinse under cold water. Drain again and set aside.

3 To make the sauce, stir to combine the Asian sesame paste, hot chili sauce, soy sauce, broth, brown sugar, and rice vinegar in a small bowl. Set aside.

4 Place a large wok or skillet over high heat for about 30 seconds. Add the peanut oil, swirl to coat the pan, and heat until hot but not smoking. Add the ground pork mixture and stir-fry vigorously, breaking up the pork into small bits. When no pink color remains on the pork, push it to one side of the wok; add the peanut oil, and then the garlic and scallions. Stir-fry for 1 to 2 minutes, until they begin to soften. Then add the cabbage. Stir-fry the cabbage, scallions, and garlic for about 2 minutes.

5 Combine the vegetables together with the pork mixture and add the sauce ingredients to the wok. Add the noodles and toss gently until the noodles and sauce are hot.

6 Place the noodles in a warm serving dish and garnish with crushed peanuts. Serve immediately.

NOTE: Asian sesame paste is a thick paste made from toasted sesame seeds. It differs from tahini, the Middle Eastern sesame paste, which is made from untoasted seeds. An opened jar of Asian sesame paste will keep indefinitely in the refrigerator, but stir well before using as the oil tends to separate out.

Peking Noodles

Chinese spaghetti with meat sauce? For pasta lovers, here's a dish that's at once familiar and exotic. The combination of hoisin sauce and hot bean sauce gives the sauce its distinctive flavor.

2 tablespoons soy sauce

2 tablespoons hoisin sauce

1 teaspoon sugar

2 teaspoons cornstarch

3/4 pound lean pork, coarsely ground or chopped

1/2 cup unsalted vegetable or chicken broth (pages 218–222)

1 1/2 tablespoons hot bean paste

1 tablespoon rice vinegar or white vinegar

1 pound fresh lo mein noodles

1 tablespoon vegetable oil

2/3 cup chopped onion (about 1 small onion)

1 large garlic clove, chopped

1 In a medium-size bowl, combine the soy sauce, hoisin sauce, sugar, and cornstarch. Add the pork and mix well. Set aside.

2 For the sauce, combine the broth, hot bean paste, and vinegar.

3 Cook the lo mein noodles in a large pot of boiling water until tender but still firm, about 5 to 7 minutes. Drain, rinse with lukewarm water, and drain again. Keep the noodles warm in a covered dish in a 200°F oven.

4 Place a wok or large skillet over high heat for 30 seconds. Add the vegetable oil, swirl to coat the pan, and heat until hot but not smoking. Add the onion and garlic and stir-fry until the onion has softened and is beginning to brown. Transfer to a serving dish.

5 Reheat the wok until it is hot but not smoking. Add the pork and

stir-fry over high heat, breaking up the pork as you cook, until the pork has browned, about 3 or 4 minutes. Add the onion and the sauce. Bring to a simmer and taste for seasoning. You may wish to add more bean sauce or hot chili oil, if you prefer a hotter dish.

6 Pour the meat sauce over the warm noodles and serve immediately.

Pork Lo Mein

Lo Mein is a Chinese classic: lo meaning mixed and mein meaning noodles. Don't think you have to follow the recipe slavishly: beef or chicken can be substituted for the pork; celery or Chinese cabbage can replace the bok choy. This can be a quick dish you mix together with items you have in your refrigerator.

8 dried shiitake mushrooms

12 ounces dried Chinese egg noodles or angel hair pasta

1 pound boneless pork loin, trimmed of fat and sliced in thin strips

4 tablespoons peanut oil

2 teaspoons minced fresh ginger

4 stalks bok choy, white stem sliced lengthwise, and leaves diagonally sliced 1-inch thick

1 cup trimmed and halved snow peas

1/2 cup julienned bamboo shoots

6 scallions, cut into 1-inch pieces

Marinade

2 tablespoons soy sauce

1 tablespoon Chinese rice wine or dry sherry

1/4 teaspoon sugar

1 tablespoon cornstarch

Sauce

1/4 cup soy sauce

1 1/2 tablespoons oyster sauce

3 tablespoons toasted sesame oil

1 cup vegetable or chicken broth (pages 218–222)

1 Cover the mushrooms with hot water and set aside to soften for 20 to 30 minutes.

2 Cook the noodles in a large pot of boiling salted water until just done, about 5 minutes. Drain and rinse under cold water. Drain again and set aside.

3 Combine the marinade ingredients in a bowl. Add the pork, mixing well with your fingers until all pieces are coated. Set aside.

4 Combine the sauce ingredients in a small bowl. Set aside.

5 Drain the mushrooms. Discard the stems and thinly slice the caps.

6 Place a wok or large skillet over high heat for about 30 seconds. Add 2 tablespoons of the peanut oil, swirl to coat the pan, and heat until hot but not smoking. Add the pork mixture and marinade; stir-fry for about 3 minutes, until the pork is no longer pink. Remove the mixture to a platter and set aside. Wipe out the wok.

7 Reheat the wok; add 2 more tablespoons of oil. Add the ginger and stir-fry for 30 seconds. Add the bok choy, snow peas, and bamboo shoots and stir-fry until the bok-choy is tender-crisp, about 3 minutes. Add the scallions and mushrooms; stir-fry for another minute. Add the reserved meat mixture, tossing lightly until heated through. Using a slotted spoon, transfer the meat and vegetables to a bowl, leaving the liquid in the wok.

8 Add the noodles and sauce to the wok. Stir over medium heat until hot. Remove to a large platter. Spoon the meat and vegetable mixture over the top. Toss together and serve immediately.

Pancit with **Pork**

Pancit is the Filipino interpretation of noodles, clearly showing the Chinese influence on their national cuisine.

8 ounces cellophane noodles or sweet potato starch noodles

6 medium-size dried shiitake mushrooms

1 tablespoon peanut or canola oil

6 ounces lean pork, cut in thin strips (3/8 by 1/4 by 2 inches)

1/4 pound chorizo sausage, sliced 1/4-inch thick (optional)

1 cup sliced onion

4 garlic cloves, minced

1 small red bell pepper, julienned

2 cups snow peas, halved

3 tablespoons mushroom soy sauce or soy sauce

1 to 1 1/2 cups chicken broth (pages 220–222)

1/2 teaspoon freshly ground black pepper

2 tablespoons sliced scallion

1 Cover the noodles with hot water and set aside to soften for 15 minutes. Drain, rinse with cold water. Scissor into 4-inch long lengths and set aside.

2 Soak the mushrooms in hot water to cover for 20 to 30 minutes. Squeeze dry and discard any stems. Quarter the mushroom caps.

3 Heat a wok or large skillet over high heat for 30 seconds. Add the oil, swirl to coat the pan, and heat until hot but not smoking. Add the pork and stir-fry for 2 minutes. Add the chorizo sausage, if using, and stir-fry for 2 minutes. Push the meat to one side of the wok.

4 Add the onion, garlic, and red bell pepper and continue stir-frying until the vegetables have wilted, about 3 minutes. Add the

mushrooms, snow peas, and soy sauce. Stir-fry the vegetables and meat all together until hot, about 1 minute. Add 1 cup of the chicken broth, the noodles, and black pepper. Continue stir-frying, adding a little more chicken broth as it is absorbed, until the vegetables are tender and the dish has absorbed most of the juices, about 4 to 5 minutes. Serve hot with scallion slices scattered over the dish.

NOTE: I have substituted chorizo sausage for the Chinese pork sausages that are more traditional. Sweet potato starch noodles also work well in this dish.

Rice Vermicelli with Pork and Porcini

The subtle flavors of the rich mushrooms, browned pork, braised cabbage, garlic, and scallions blend and are absorbed by the noodles in this aromatic dish. The full-bodied mushroom flavor of the porcini mushroom soaking liquid adds immeasurably to the finished stir-fry.

1 ounce dried sliced porcini mushrooms

6 ounces rice vermicelli

2 tablespoons peanut or canola oil

1 teaspoon toasted sesame oil

3/4 pound boneless pork, thinly sliced, then cut in 1 1/2-inch strips

1 large garlic clove, minced

4 or 5 large scallions, including some green parts, julienned (about 1 cup)

6 ounces portobello mushrooms, stems discarded, caps halved and thinly sliced, or brown crimini mushrooms, thinly sliced

4 cups shredded Napa cabbage

Approximately 2 tablespoons mushroom soy sauce, tamari, or soy sauce

1/2 cup chopped water chestnuts or daikon radish

1/2 cup snow pea shoots, cut in 1/2-inch lengths (optional)

Freshly ground black pepper

1   Cover the dried porcini mushrooms with hot water and let soak for 20 to 30 minutes. Drain and save the soaking liquid. Rinse the mushrooms and squeeze dry.

2   Cover the rice vermicelli with boiling water and let soak for 15 minutes until softened. Untangle the noodles with your fingers and drain.

3   Place a wok or large skillet over high heat for 30 seconds. Add 2 teaspoons of the peanut oil and the toasted sesame oil, swirl to

coat the pan, and heat until hot but not smoking. Add the pork strips and stir-fry for 2 minutes, until no pink remains. Remove to a dish and set aside.

4   Add the remaining peanut oil to the skillet or wok. When hot, add the garlic and scallions and stir-fry until wilted. Add the fresh mushrooms and stir-fry until softened, adding a little mushroom liquid as needed for dryness. Add the cabbage and continue stir-frying, adding small amounts of mushroom liquid and soy sauce as needed.

5   When the cabbage has wilted completely, start adding the drained noodles, a few handfuls at a time, adding small amounts of mushroom liquid and soy sauce as you stir-fry. Expect to have extra mushroom liquid.

6   Add the water chestnuts, snow pea shoots, if using, and the pork. Grind black pepper over the dish and taste for seasoning. You may wish to add more soy sauce. Serve immediately.

NOTE: For this recipe, a noodle that is a little thicker than normal gives the best results. I look for Golden Sail Dongguan Rick Stick from the People's Republic of China.

Stir-Fried Pork with Glass Noodles

YIELD: 4 MAIN-COURSE SERVINGS

The crunchy stir-fried vegetables and browned pork contrast nicely with the warm, loosely set eggs and soft noodles in this dish.

4 (1.75-ounce) skeins cellophane noodles

2 tablespoons toasted sesame oil

1 tablespoon minced garlic

1/2 pound boneless pork, sliced 3/8-inch thick, then cut in 1/2- by 3-inch strips

2 carrots, julienned

4 cups thinly sliced Napa cabbage

3/4 cup sliced scallions (3/4-inch length)

2 tablespoons Asian fish sauce

1 teaspoon freshly ground black pepper

2 eggs, beaten

1 1/2 cups mung bean sprouts

Garnish: Cilantro sprigs

Soy Lime Dipping Sauce (page 207) or Nuoc Cham (page 208)

1 Cover the cellophane noodles with hot tap water and set aside to soften for 15 minutes. Drain the noodles, rinse with cold water, and drain again. Scissor into 3-inch lengths and set aside.

2 Place a wok or large skillet over high heat for 30 seconds. Add 1 tablespoon of the sesame oil, swirl to coat the pan, and heat until hot but not smoking. Add the garlic and stir-fry about 30 seconds. Add the pork and stir-fry about 3 minutes, until the pork has slightly browned. Remove the pork with a slotted spoon and set aside. Add the remaining 1 tablespoon sesame oil and heat through. Then add the carrots, cabbage, and scallions and stir-fry until the vegetables begin to soften, about 5 minutes. Add the noodles, fish sauce, and black pepper; stir-fry for 1 minute until heated.

3 Make a hole in the center of the stir-fry and pour the eggs into it. Stir the eggs gently until loosely set. Then stir them into the noodles. Stir in the bean sprouts and cook until the dish is heated through. Serve hot, garnished with cilantro sprigs, with Soy Lime Dipping Sauce or Nuoc Cham on the side.

Tamarind Pork Stir-Fry on **Noodle Cake**

YIELD: 4 MAIN-COURSE SERVINGS

Tamarind has a piquant sweet-and-sour taste that melds beautifully with pork. This dish is quite striking served on a very large round platter, with the colors of the yellow noodle cake, deep brown tamarind sauce, and dark green spinach leaves.

Two-Sides Brown Noodlecake (page 119)

2 tablespoons peanut or corn oil

2 teaspoons minced fresh ginger

2 teaspoons minced garlic

1/4 cup shallots

3/4 pound boneless pork, sliced in 3/8-inch strips

1/4 pound fresh shiitakes, or portobello mushrooms, stems removed, caps sliced 3/8-inch thick

6 ounces fresh spinach leaves, washed and stems removed (about 1 1/2 quarts, lightly packed)

Sauce

3 tablespoons tamarind purée (pages 16-17)

2 tablespoons hoisin sauce

1/2 cup vegetable or chicken broth (pages 218–222)

2 teaspoons cornstarch dissolved in 2 teaspoons water

Freshly ground black pepper

1 Prepare the noodles according to the recipe directions. Keep warm in a 200°F oven.

2 Place a wok or large skillet over high heat for 30 seconds. Add the oil, swirl to coat the pan, and heat until hot but not smoking. Add the ginger, garlic, and shallots and stir-fry over medium high heat for 2 minutes, until softened. Push the mixture to one side and add the pork. Stir-fry over high heat for 3 minutes. Add the mushrooms and continue stir-frying for 2 minutes. Add the spinach leaves and stir-fry for 1 minute. Spoon the mixture onto the center of the warm noodle cake.

3　Stir together the sauce ingredients and add them to the wok. Bring them to a boil, stirring, for 1 minute. Pour the sauce over the stir-fry in the center of the noodle cake. Serve hot.

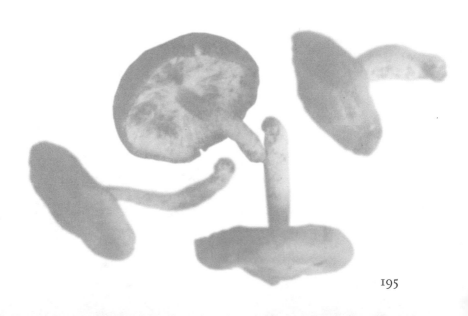

Yaki-Soba

A delectable combination of browned soba noodles, thin slices of beef, big slices of soft onion and shiitakes, and sliced water spinach.

> 5 medium-size dried shiitake mushrooms
>
> 10 to 12 ounces dried soba noodles
>
> 3 tablespoons vegetable oil
>
> 8 to 10 ounces beef sirloin
>
> Salt and freshly ground black pepper
>
> 1 medium onion, slivered into 1/2-inch slices
>
> 1 teaspoon minced fresh ginger
>
> 1/4 pound Asian water spinach or Western spinach, stems removed and sliced 3/4-inch thick
>
> Approximately 3 tablespoons mushroom soy sauce or soy sauce

1 Soak the mushrooms in hot water to cover for 20 to 30 minutes. Drain and squeeze dry. Discard the stems and thinly slice the caps.

2 Cook the soba noodles in a large pot of boiling salted water over high heat until just done, about 5 to 7 minutes. Drain well. Or, to cook by the *sashimizu* method, bring a large pot of water to a boil. Add the noodles and cook for 2 minutes. Add 1 cup of cold water and return to a boil. Repeat the process twice. Simmer the noodles until tender, about 5 minutes. Drain well. Toss with 1 tablespoon of the oil and set aside.

3 Cut the beef across the grain into 1-inch strips. Turn each strip 90° on its side. Then cut the strips across the grain into 1/4-inch slices. Cut these long thin slices into 1-inch pieces (quarter size).

4 Heat a wok or large skillet over high heat for 30 seconds. Add 2 teaspoons of oil, swirl to coat the pan, and heat until very hot but not smoking. Add half the beef and stir-fry for 2 to 3 minutes until just done. Remove the beef to a serving dish. Add 2 teaspoons of

oil and brown the remainder of the beef. Remove to a serving dish and season with salt and black pepper.

5 Reheat the wok. Add the onion and ginger and stir-fry for 2 to 3 minutes until the onion has softened slightly. Add the mushrooms and spinach and stir-fry for 2 minutes. Remove to the serving dish.

6 Reheat the wok over high heat, adding a little oil if necessary. Fry the noodles in 2 or 3 batches, shaking a few teaspoons of soy sauce over them as they cook until they are slightly browned. This will take about 3 minutes per batch. Add the beef and vegetables to the last batch of noodles when they are browned and stir-fry for a minute.

7 Toss all the noodles and vegetables together. Taste for seasoning; it may need more black pepper or soy sauce. Serve hot.

NOTE: I particularly like Superior brand mushroom soy sauce added to the soba when browning them. It has a good flavor for this dish and seems to help with the browning. The beef and the noodles are browned in two batches so that they brown properly. Each piece of food must come into direct contact with the pan to brown. With too much in the pan, you get stewing and steaming, instead of sizzling and browning.

Stir-Fried Beef and Ramen Noodles

YIELD: 4 MAIN-COURSE SERVINGS

This is a good basic stir-fry. The concentrated flavor of the dried mushrooms adds immeasurably to the dish.

1 ounce dried porcini mushrooms or dried shiitake mushrooms

10 or 11 ounces dried ramen noodles (or 3 small packages of ramen instant soup noodles, seasoning packet discarded)

1 teaspoon toasted sesame oil

1 tablespoon plus 2 teaspoons peanut or corn oil

8 ounces sirloin or chuck steak, fat removed, julienned

2 garlic cloves, minced

1 cup thinly sliced sweet onion or red onion (1 medium-size onion)

1/2 pound Napa cabbage, stem section removed, leaves julienned (about 4 cups)

2 tablespoons mushroom soy sauce or soy sauce

Freshly ground black pepper

1 Soak the dried mushrooms in the hot water for 20 to 30 minutes. Drain, saving the soaking liquid. Rinse the mushrooms thoroughly to remove any dirt or sand. Squeeze the mushrooms dry and thinly slice. Set aside.

2 Cook the ramen noodles in a large pot of boiling water until just done, about 2 to 3 minutes. Drain and rinse under cold water. Drain well, and toss with the sesame oil.

3 Heat a wok or large skillet over high heat for 30 seconds. Add 2 teaspoons of the peanut oil, swirl to coat the pan, and heat until hot but not smoking. Add half the beef and stir-fry for 2 to 3 until the meat just changes color. Remove the beef to a serving dish. Add 2 teaspoons oil and repeat with the remaining beef. Add to the serving dish and set aside.

4 Reheat the wok and add the remaining 1 teaspoon oil, swirling to

coat the pan. Add the garlic, onion, and cabbage. Stir-fry for 2 or 3 minutes, until the vegetables have softened. Add the mushrooms and soy sauce and cook for about 1 minute, until the mushrooms and vegetables are cooked. Add the noodles and the reserved mushroom liquid. Toss for a minute or two. Add the beef and black pepper. Toss until hot. Serve at once, with soy sauce on the side.

VARIATION: Chicken, pork, or tofu may be substituted for the beef.

Aromatic Beef and Noodles with Simmered Greens

YIELD: 4 MAIN-COURSE SERVINGS

Simmering the greens with the noodles works out well in this gutsy, lightly spiced dish, since the remaining cooking can be done in the wok. If you have never had Chinese broccoli, it is well worth searching it out for its delicious flavor. The stems have the texture of asparagus.

8 dried shiitake mushrooms

3 tablespoons soy sauce

1 tablespoon minced garlic

1 tablespoon cornstarch

1 pound boneless sirloin, tender chuck, or flank steak, sliced in thin strips across the grain

2 tablespoons oyster sauce

1 teaspoon chili paste with garlic (or more to taste)

1 cup beef broth

12 ounces fresh or dried Chinese wheat flour noodles or dried fettuccine or linguine

1 pound Chinese broccoli, stems cut diagonally 1-inch thick, or bok choy cut in 2-inch pieces

3 tablespoons peanut oil

2 cinnamon sticks, broken in half

1 teaspoon aniseed

1 tablespoon chopped fresh ginger

6 to 8 scallions, including the green parts, cut in 1-inch pieces

1 Cover the mushrooms with hot water and set aside for 20 to 30 minutes.

2 Combine the soy sauce, garlic, and cornstarch in a medium-size bowl. Add the beef, mixing well with your fingers until all the pieces are coated.

3 Combine the oyster sauce, chili paste, and beef broth in a small bowl and set aside.

4 Drain the mushrooms. Discard the stems and thinly slice the caps.

5 Bring 5 quarts of water to a boil. Add the noodles and simmer for about 5 minutes until the noodles begin to soften. Add the greens to the noodles and cook briefly until the greens and pasta are tender. Drain well and turn into a serving dish.

6 While the noodles simmer, place a wok or large skillet over high heat for 30 seconds. Add 2 tablespoons of the oil, swirl to coat the pan, and heat until hot but not smoking. Add the beef mixture and stir-fry for about 2 minutes, just until the beef slices have lost their red color. Remove the beef to a platter and set aside. Wipe out the wok.

7 Reheat the wok with the remaining 1 tablespoon of oil. Add the cinnamon sticks, aniseed, ginger, and scallions. Stir-fry over medium heat for 2 minutes. Add the mushrooms and beef broth mixture and bring to a boil for 2 minutes.

8 Add the beef to the sauce and heat for a minute. Pour the beef and sauce over the greens and pasta. Toss gently, remove the cinnamon sticks and serve hot.

Char Siu Noodle Stir-Fry

YIELD: 4 MAIN-COURSE SERVINGS

This dish can be varied depending on what fresh vegetables you have on hand. The Chinese roast pork can be homemade or purchased at a Chinese grocery. You can even substitute leftover cooked chicken, beef, or pork.

4 to 5 dried shiitake mushrooms

12 ounces fresh thin (1/8-inch) Chinese egg noodles

2 teaspoons toasted sesame oil

1/3 cup vegetable or chicken broth (pages 218–222)

3 tablespoons soy sauce

1 teaspoon sugar

1/2 teaspoon freshly ground black pepper

1 1/2 tablespoons peanut or canola oil

2 teaspoons minced fresh ginger

2 garlic cloves, minced

2 scallions, white and green parts, diagonally sliced in 1-inch pieces

1 small sweet red bell pepper, julienned

1 small zucchini, halved and sliced

1 small yellow squash, halved and sliced

6 ounces Chinese Roast Pork (page 204), halved and sliced

1   In a small bowl, soak the dried mushrooms in warm water for 20 minutes or more. Drain, squeeze dry, and slice the caps. Discard the stems.

2   To a large pot of salted boiling water, add the Chinese egg noodles, and over high heat return to a boil. Test the noodles at this point. They should be done. Drain and rinse in cold water. Drain well and toss with sesame oil. Set aside.

3   In a small bowl, combine the broth, soy sauce, sugar, and black pepper.

4 Place a wok or large skillet over high heat for 30 seconds. Add the oil, swirl to coat the pan, and heat until hot but not smoking. Add the ginger, garlic, and scallions and stir-fry for 1 minute. Add the shiitakes, red bell pepper, zucchini, and yellow squash and stir-fry until the vegetables have softened, about 4 minutes. Add the pork and the sauce. Toss well to combine. Add the noodles and toss gently until the noodles are hot and have absorbed the sauce. Serve immediately.

Chinese Roast Pork (CHAR SIU)

YIELD: 6 MAIN-COURSE SERVINGS

Chinese Roast Pork is a versatile ingredient to have on hand for stir-fried dishes or sliced to go with a meal. Add the pork to a Sichuan Noodle Salad (page 56) or Char Sui Noodle Stir-Fry (page 202). A good-tasting hoisin sauce is critical to the outcome of this dish, but hoisin sauces very greatly. An excellent brand is Koon Chun Hoisin, which can be found in Asian groceries.

2 pork tenderloins, 2 to 2 1/2 pounds total

3 tablespoons hoisin sauce

6 tablespoons honey

1 tablespoon preserved red bean curd or 1 teaspoon five-spice powder and 1/2 teaspoon minced fresh ginger

2 tablespoons sugar

2 tablespoons tomato catsup

1 tablespoon rice wine or dry sherry

1 tablespoon minced garlic

1 Slice each pork tenderloin in half lengthwise.

2 In a small bowl, combine the hoisin sauce, 4 tablespoons of the honey, preserved red bean curd or spice substitutes, sugar, catsup, rice wine, and garlic. Pour over the pork and marinate in a large zippered plastic bag, turning to coat all surfaces of the pork, for at least an hour, or overnight.

3 Preheat the oven to 375°F. Line a roasting pan with foil. Place the meat on an oiled wire rack in the foil-lined pan. Pour 1/2 cup water in the roasting pan. Roast for 30 minutes, basting every 15 minutes and adding more water as needed. Turn the pork and roast for another 30 minutes, basting every 15 minutes and adding more water as needed.

4 When the pork is done, brush the meat with the remaining 2 tablespoons of honey and let cool.

A Few Basic Stocks and Sauces

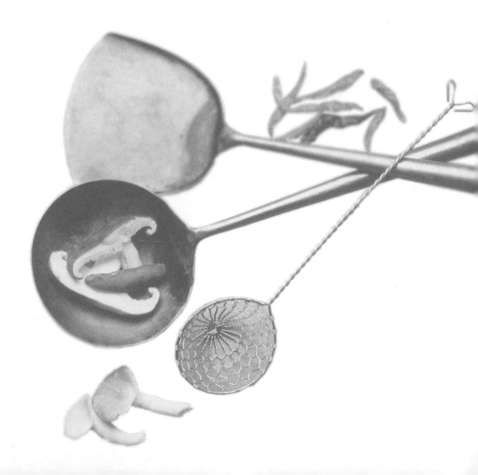

Soy Ginger Dipping Sauce

A basic soy-based dipping sauce for dumplings.

> 6 tablespoons soy sauce
>
> 1 tablespoon rice wine or dry sherry
>
> 1 tablespoon grated fresh ginger

1 Combine all the ingredients in a small bowl and mix well. The sauce may be stored in an airtight jar in the refrigerator for up to a month.

Soy Lime Dipping Sauce

Y IELD: 3/4 CUP

This sauce has more depth and more spice than Soy Ginger Dipping Sauce (page 206). It is also a good choice for serving with dumplings and spring rolls.

1/3 cup soy sauce

2 teaspoons chili paste with garlic

1 teaspoon minced ginger

1/4 cup fresh lime juice with pulp

2 teaspoons sugar

2 tablespoons water

1 scallion, including the green part, minced

2 tablespoons chopped cilantro leaves

1 Combine all the ingredients in a glass jar and stir to dissolve the sugar. The sauce may be stored in an airtight jar in the refrigerator for up to 2 weeks.

NOTE: The lime pulp adds a lot to this versatile sauce. After juicing the limes, scrape out some of the pulp with a teaspoon.

Nuoc Cham

This is the classic Vietnamese dipping sauce. A little bit goes a long way. It is perishable, and leftovers should not be saved.

1 1/2 tablespoons sugar

1/4 cup water

1 tablespoon Asian fish sauce

Juice of 1 lime

1 garlic clove, minced

1/4 teaspoon crushed red pepper

1   In a small saucepan, combine the sugar and water. Heat until the sugar dissolves. Cool, then add the remaining ingredients and mix well. Serve at room temperature.

Southeast Asian Sweet and **Sour Sauce**

YIELD: ABOUT 1/2 CUP

Don't let the brief ingredients list fool you: This is a great sauce with the flavors in perfect harmony.

1/4 cup sugar

1/4 cup water

1 1/2 teaspoons Asian fish sauce

1 tablespoon fresh lime juice

1 Combine the sugar and water in a small saucepan. Place over medium heat until the sugar dissolves, about 3 minutes. Remove from the heat and cool to room temperature. Add the fish sauce and lemon juice and serve.

Ginger Apricot Sauce

YIELD: 1 CUP

A delightful sauce with pork dumplings or duck dishes.

1/2 cup dried apricots (about 3 ounces)

1/4 cup crystallized ginger (about 1 ounce)

2 tablespoons brown sugar

2 tablespoons fresh lemon or lime juice

3/4 cup water

2 teaspoons rice vinegar

1 tablespoon honey

1 tablespoon hoisin sauce

1 In a small nonreactive saucepan, simmer the apricots, crystallized ginger, sugar, lemon juice, and water for 5 minutes, until the apricots have softened.

2 Transfer the ingredients to a mini food processor or blender. Add the vinegar, honey, and hoisin sauce and process until mostly, but not completely, smooth. Serve at room temperature. Store leftovers in an airtight container in the refrigerator for up to 6 weeks.

Chili Dipping Sauce

YIELD: ABOUT 1 CUP

The heat of this dipping sauce depends on the chiles you choose. For a mild sauce, don't include the seeds of the chiles.

1/2 cup minced fresh red or green chile peppers

2 large garlic cloves, minced

2 tablespoons minced fresh ginger

2 tablespoons soy sauce

1 tablespoon brown sugar

1 teaspoon salt

1/3 cup rice vinegar

2 tablespoons water

1 Combine all the ingredients in a small nonreactive saucepan. Bring to a boil, reduce the heat, and simmer for 5 minutes, until the sauce has thickened slightly. Serve at room temperature. Store leftovers in an airtight container in the refrigerator for up to 6 months.

Toasted Sesame Sauce

This is a great sauce. It can be used as a dip for egg rolls or as a basting liquid for a roast chicken or salmon.

1/4 cup unhulled sesame seeds

2 tablespoons toasted sesame oil

1/3 cup soy sauce

1/4 cup rice vinegar

1 tablespoon mirin

1 Toast the sesame seeds in a large nonstick skillet over medium heat, shaking the pan frequently, for 5 minutes or more, until they are aromatic and are just beginning to brown.

2 In a mini food processor or with a mortar and pestle, crush the sesame seeds. Add the toasted sesame oil, then the soy sauce, vinegar, and mirin. Blend well. The sauce will keep refrigerated, in a tightly closed container, for 6 to 8 weeks.

Cashew Sauce

YIELD: ABOUT 1/2 CUP

This mildly sweet rich sauce is delightful with dumplings, spring rolls, or deep-fried wontons. For the best flavor, make this sauce ahead.

1/3 cup cashew butter

1/2 teaspoon minced ginger

1/4 teaspoon minced garlic

1/2 teaspoon chili paste with garlic

1/4 teaspoon light brown sugar

1 teaspoon rice vinegar

1 teaspoon soy sauce

1/4 cup vegetable or chicken broth (pages 218–222)

1   In a small bowl, combine the cashew butter, ginger, garlic, chili paste with garlic, sugar, vinegar, and soy sauce. Heat the broth and whisk into the cashew mixture. Taste for spiciness and salt, and adjust seasonings. Serve at room temperature. Store leftovers in an airtight container in the refrigerator for 1 to 2 days.

VARIATION: Substitute a natural peanut butter for the cashew butter, or grind your own roasted peanuts in a food processor.

Asian Pesto Sauce

YIELD: ABOUT 2 CUPS

I enjoy using different herbs in my pestos—several years ago I wrote an entire book devoted to pestos made of all different herbs (entitled Pestos!). In this recipe, the herbal trinity of Southeast Asian cooking— cilantro, basil, and mint—are made into a light pesto, with coconut milk binding the mixture in much the same way that olive oil binds the traditional Genoese basil pesto.

3/4 cup coconut milk

2 tablespoons lime juice

1 cup fresh cilantro leaves, including some stems

1/2 cup fresh Thai or sweet basil leaves, including some stems

1/2 cup fresh mint leaves

1/4 cup chopped scallion

1/4 cup roasted unsalted peanuts

1/2 green chile, such as jalapeño, serrano or Thai bird chile, seeded

1 teaspoon grated lime zest

1 large garlic clove, roughly chopped

1/2 teaspoon sugar

1/2 teaspoon salt

1 teaspoon freshly ground white or black pepper

1   In a blender or food processor, combine the coconut milk, lime juice, cilantro, basil, mint, scallion, peanuts, chile pepper, lime zest, garlic, sugar, salt and pepper to taste. Blend to a sauce with texture. Use at once to capture the fresh herbal flavor of the sauce.

NOTES: Use this sauce, just as you would an Italian pesto sauce—toss it with still-hot just-cooked noodles for an instant main course.

Dashi

YIELD: ABOUT 4 CUPS

This mild-flavored stock is the basis for countless Japanese soups and sauces. It is made from dried kelp (kombu) and dried bonito flakes, both of which are available wherever Japanese foods are sold, including many health food stores.

3 pieces kombu (kelp), each 5 to 6 inches in length, lightly wiped with a damp cloth

4 1/2 cups spring water or good-tasting tap water

1/2 cup dried bonito flakes

1 teaspoon soy sauce

1 teaspoon salt

1 In a medium-size pan, combine the kelp and water and heat over medium-low heat for about 10 minutes, just until the stock almost reaches the boiling point. Remove the kelp from the water immediately, before the water boils. Add the dried bonito flakes, stir, and remove from the heat. Allow to steep for 5 minutes.

2 Strain the broth through a fine strainer, or a strainer lined with cheesecloth or a coffee filter. Do not press the bonito flakes when straining. Add the soy sauce and salt. The broth may be used at once or refrigerated for up to a week.

NOTE: Bottled dashi concentrate and instant dashi granules are sold in health food stores and wherever Japanese foods are sold. They make a handy alternative to homemade dashi—but, as always, homemade has the best flavor.

Basil Lemongrass Sauce

YIELD: 1 CUP

Lemongrass has a distinctly delicate flavor that is difficult to capture in a sauce. When the lemongrass stalks are dry, signaling that they have been harvested many weeks ago, the flavor is even more elusive. In this sauce, the stalks are briefly braised to bring out their flavor and soften them, then puréed in a blender. Basil Lemongrass Sauce makes a delightful accompaniment for Green Glass Noodle-Stuffed Chicken Breasts (page 174). You can also serve it with shrimp pot stickers or steamed asparagus.

1 teaspoon canola oil

1/4 cup chopped fresh or frozen lemongrass (2 stalks), using only the white lower section

1 tablespoon sugar

1/3 cup plus 1 tablespoon water

3 tablespoons fresh lemon juice

1/4 cup julienned basil leaves

1/8 teaspoon salt

1 tablespoon shiro (white) miso

2/3 cup hot water

2 teaspoons cornstarch dissolved in 1 tablespoon water

1/8 teaspoon toasted sesame oil

White pepper

1   In a small saucepan, heat the canola oil for 30 seconds. Add the lemongrass, sugar, and 1 tablespoon of water. Sauté, stirring until softened, for 3 or 4 minutes. Remove from the heat and add 1/3 cup of water, the lemon juice, 1 tablespoon chopped basil leaves, and salt. Purée the sauce in a blender, scraping down the sides.

2   In a small saucepan, dissolve the miso in 2/3 cup of hot water. Bring to a simmer and, stirring, add the cornstarch mixture to thicken. Remove from the heat and cool slightly.

3 Add the puréed blender ingredients, toasted sesame oil, and the remaining chopped basil to the miso. Grind a little white pepper into the sauce. Taste for seasoning. Serve at room temperature. The sauce will keep refrigerated for 5 days, or frozen for up to 2 months.

NOTE: Scissoring the basil leaves is easy and makes a clean cut. Shiro miso is called "white miso" but it is actually golden in color.

Asian Vegetable Broth

YIELD: 4 PINTS

There is nothing like a good stock for a wonderful soup.

1/2 ounce Chinese dried mushrooms (about 2/3 cup)

1 1/2 tablespoons peanut oil

1 large onion, peeled and chopped

2 leeks, lower 4 inches only, chopped

4 large garlic cloves, crushed

2 celery ribs with leaves, chopped

2 carrots, sliced

1/4 cup sliced fresh ginger

1 stalk lemongrass, chopped

1 teaspoon black peppercorns

2 bay leaves

1 star anise

2 teaspoons salt (optional)

2 quarts water

1 In a small bowl, cover the Chinese dried mushrooms with warm water to cover and let stand for 20 minutes or more. Save the liquid for the broth.

2 Heat the peanut oil in a large stockpot over medium heat and sauté the onion, leeks, garlic, celery, and carrots, stirring frequently, until the vegetables have softened and begun to brown. Add the remaining ingredients and bring to a rapid boil. Reduce the heat and simmer, covered, for 45 minutes.

3 Strain the broth through a large strainer or colander, pressing hard on the vegetables to extract as much liquid as possible. Discard the vegetables and spices. The broth may be used at once or refrigerated for up to a week or frozen for up to 3 months.

Garlic Broth

The combination of roasted garlic and miso gives the broth full-bodied flavor.

3 large whole garlic bulbs

9 cups water

3 tablespoons shiro (white) miso

1/2 teaspoon freshly ground black pepper

1 teaspoon salt

1   Preheat the oven to 375°F.

2   Remove the outside papery skin from the garlic, but keep the bulbs whole. Slice each bulb in half, horizontally, and fit back together. Place the garlic bulbs in a small baking dish or pie plate and add 1 tablespoon of water. Cover with foil and bake in the middle of the oven for 45 to 60 minutes, until the cloves are very soft. Remove and let cool a little.

3   In a large saucepan, heat 4 cups water and stir in the miso. Squeeze the garlic paste from the cloves into the miso broth. Add black pepper and salt and the remaining 5 cups water. Simmer, uncovered, for 30 minutes. Purée the garlic broth in a blender on high speed. Taste for seasoning.

4   The broth may be used at once or refrigerated for up to a week or frozen for up to 3 months.

Homemade Chicken Broth

YIELD: 16 CUPS

This classic chicken broth is simmered for 3 hours to develop body and flavor. The salt is omitted, so that the broth may be used in a sauce or reduction later.

3 pounds chicken wings

4 quarts cold water

1 carrot, roughly chopped

1 small onion, thinly sliced

2 celery ribs, including leaves, chopped

2 large scallions, roughly chopped

1 teaspoon black peppercorns

1 Rinse the chicken wings under cold water. Place in a large heavy soup pot. Add the cold water and place over high heat. Bring to a very low boil. Skim off the foam and particles that rise to the surface. After the surface is clear, add the carrot, onion, celery, scallions, and peppercorns. Continue cooking at a low simmer, partially covered, for 3 hours or more. Do not let the broth boil and do not stir.

2 Strain the chicken broth through several layers of dampened cheesecloth or a clean kitchen dish towel. Discard the solids. Cool to room temperature, then chill in the refrigerator. After the broth has chilled, spoon off the layer of hard fat on the surface. The chicken broth may be stored in the refrigerator for a day or two, or frozen for up to 3 months.

Lemony Chicken Broth

YIELD: ABOUT 4 CUPS

This simple broth is quick and easy, best if made with homemade chicken broth. But if I am short on time, I use a canned broth and it is still delicious.

1 tablespoon peanut oil

1 tablespoon minced garlic

1/4 cup minced shallots

2 quarter-size slices fresh ginger, smashed

5 cups chicken broth (pages 220–222)

1 stalk fresh lemongrass, trimmed of outer leaves, pounded and cut into 2-inch pieces (optional)

1 to 1 1/2 tablespoons fresh lemon or lime juice

Salt and freshly ground black pepper to taste

1 In a large saucepan, heat the peanut oil over medium heat until hot but not smoking. Add the garlic, shallots, and ginger. Stir-fry for 2 minutes. Add the chicken broth and bring to a boil. Simmer for 30 minutes, adding the lemongrass, if using, after 15 minutes. Remove from the heat. Strain the broth, discarding the solids. Add the lemon or lime juice and salt and black pepper to taste. The broth may be used at once, or refrigerated for a day or two, or frozen for up to 3 months.

Speedy Broth

While a slow-cooked chicken broth will have a richer flavor, there is still a place for a quicker homemade broth which provides more flavor than the canned variety.

3 pounds chicken wings or 1 small chicken, 3 to 4 pounds, cut in small pieces

4 quarts water

1 carrot, roughly chopped

1 onion, roughly chopped

2 celery ribs, roughly chopped

1 teaspoon black peppercorns

1   Rinse the chicken pieces under cold water. In a large stockpot, bring the chicken pieces and water to a simmer. Skim off the foam and particles that rise to the surface. Add the remaining ingredients and simmer for about 40 minutes until the chicken is tender. Do not let the broth boil and do not stir. Remove the chicken pieces and reserve for other use. Continue simmering the broth for another 15 minutes.

2   Strain the broth, discarding the solids. The broth is ready to use, or it can be refrigerated for a few days, or frozen for up to 3 months.

Hot Chili Oil

YIELD: 1 3/4 CUPS

This flavored oil can add tremendous flavor to any dish in which it is used. Use freshly ground chile flakes—not ones that have sat on a store shelf or your spice cupboard for several months. I don't strain the chili oil because the sediment that settles to the bottom of the jar is so good to cook with.

> 1/3 cup dried red chile flakes
>
> 1 1/2 cups peanut or corn oil
>
> 1/4 cup toasted sesame oil
>
> 1 tablespoon minced fresh ginger

1 Combine the red chile flakes, peanut oil, toasted sesame oil, and ginger in a small, heavy nonreactive saucepan. Using a deep-fry thermometer, heat the oil to 225°F, stirring at intervals. Chili oil is easy to burn at this stage, as the heat rises very quickly as it nears 200°F. Simmer at 225°F for 10 minutes, keeping a close watch on the thermometer. Remove from the heat and set aside until cool.

2 Store in a glass container in a cool dark cupboard for up to 1 year.

Homemade Curry Paste

YIELD: 2/3 CUP

This aromatic paste has more intense flavors than a dry curry powder.

2 tablespoons chopped fresh ginger

1 tablespoon chopped garlic

1/4 cup chopped shallots

2 stalks chopped fresh lemongrass (tender inner portion of lower stalk) or 1/4 cup frozen chopped lemongrass or 1 tablespoon grated lime

1 teaspoon crushed red pepper flakes

2 tablespoons ground coriander

1 tablespoon ground cumin

1 teaspoon turmeric

2 teaspoons ground cardamom

1 tablespoon freshly ground white or black pepper

1 teaspoon salt

3 tablespoons lime or lemon juice

1 Combine all the ingredients in a blender or food processor and purée into a rough paste. Refrigerate, tightly sealed, for a week, or freeze for 6 to 8 weeks.

Mail Order Sources of Ingredients

Most of the ingredients used in this book are available in supermarkets and health food stores. Some of the ingredients can only be found in a specialty store that caters to an Asian population. If you don't live near such a store, you can find everything you need through the mail.

Adriana's Caravan
409 Vanderbilt St.
Brooklyn, NY 11218
800-316-0820
718-436-8565

Anzen Importers
736 N.E. Union Ave.
Portland, OR 97232
503-233-5111

The CMC Company
PO Box 322
Avalon, NJ 08202
800-CMC-2780
http://clever.net/wwwmall/cmc

Oriental Food Mkt. & Cooking School
2801 W. Howard St.
Chicago, IL 60645
312-274-2826

Uwajimaya
519 Sixth Avenue S.
Seattle WA 98104
206-624-6248

Vietnam Imports
922 W. Broad St.
Falls Church, VA 22046
703-534-9441

Index

BOOKS BY THE CROSSING PRESS

Bill Taylor Cooks Chicken
By Bill Taylor

As former Corporate Chef at The Crossing Press, Bill Taylor has prepared hundreds of chicken dishes and has chosen the very best for this book. "I watch the fat content of every dish I prepare and find that people don't really miss the fat as long as the food is tasty. On this score, I get feedback after every meal and the votes are clearly in—people here really like the way I cook."

$12.95 • Paper • ISBN 1-58091-045-9

Everyday Tofu: From Pancakes to Pizza

By Gary Landgrebe

This book offers all Americans an opportunity to incorporate tofu into their everyday diets. We are not asking them to change their habits. We say sincerely that Americans who have remained aloof from the tofu craze will honestly be pleased by these recipes which combine tofu with their favorite foods and seasonings to create Western style main dishes, breads, and desserts.

$12.95 • Paper • ISBN 1-58091-047-5

Japanese Vegetarian Cooking
By Patricia Richfield

Easy-to-follow directions, information on techniques, plus a glossary of Japanese ingredients make this a must-have cookbook for all Japanese food fans.

$14.95 • Paper • ISBN 0-89594-805-2

Salad Dressings

By Teresa H. Burns

This little book is full of creative dressings that are fresh, healthy and delicious.

$6.95 • Paper • ISBN 0-89594-895-8

To receive a current catalog from The Crossing Press
please call toll-free, 800-777-1048.
Visit our Web site: www.crossingpress.com